Corporate Executive Protection:

An Introduction for Corporations and Security Professionals

Christian West
and
Brian Jantzen

Corporate Executive Protection:
An Introduction for Corporations and Security Professionals

© 2016 AS Solution

The topics discussed in this book represent the opinions and personal judgments of the authors and of professionals with whom they consulted in the course of preparing this work. As each situation encountered by the protection professional will vary, so necessarily will the appropriate response. As the specific policies and procedures to be followed by individual professionals may vary according to the laws of each state, the conscientious professional should consult with legal counsel before adopting guidelines and procedures.

ISBN 978-1-5323-0828-4

AS SOLUTION™
FORWARD THINKING

Published by AS Solution

Bellevue, Washington, USA

A must-read book for anyone involved in executive protection. Everyone from CSOs to principals and providers should be familiar with these guidelines. The safeguarding of people in corporate contexts is probed in a way that clearly illustrates the essential ingredients of this emerging new profession. Thanks to the authors for showing how executive protection can preclude business interruptions and might even save a life.

Stevan J. Bernard
CSO

Executive protection differs greatly from other corporate activities. However, to succeed, a corporate EP effort must fit well with corporate culture and structure. This book lays out a path for starting, redesigning, refining, and sustaining corporate EP programs. Especially useful are its case studies that depict EP methods in the real world, as well as EP staff interaction with corporate clients.

Robert L. Oatman, CPP
President
R. L. Oatman & Associates, Inc.

Christian West and Brian Jantzen convincingly highlight the multidimensional aspects of delivering first-class corporate executive protection. Doing the job right requires more than just personal security. Christian and Brian grasp the notion that high-quality executive protection is really about delivering full-client service. That means enhancing executive and corporate productivity by tailoring efforts to the individual needs of the principal as well as other corporate stakeholders.

Dannie Bergmann
Security Director, Chairman's Office
Alibaba

Foreword

Charles Randolph
Senior Director–Executive Protection,
Event Risk Management and Intelligence
Microsoft

Of Protectors and Programs

Arguably, the business world has been globalizing since just after World War I, which began ironically with the assassination of Archduke Franz Ferdinand of Austria. It is believed that ultimately his protective operation (or lack thereof) failed him, and so began the Great War. During this new era, companies would become multinational entities. As a result, the need to explore and develop business and marketplaces continued to be forefront in the minds of senior executives. While moving into new areas to conduct business operations or sales can be invigorating to the bottom line, it can also be fraught with risk and, sometimes, downright dangerous. Enter the protector.

Whether through corporate mandate, executive perk, or apparent necessity, the protector's aim is to keep the "designate" safe and secure within available means. Sometimes protective operations are formed due to the tyranny of the immediate, based on some event or issue which requires a layer of security to be formed and organized around an executive or company leaders immediately. Other times, efforts are manifested based on benchmarking or an understanding of a need. While the traditional role of the bodyguard remains at the heart of a close protection program, it has evolved into an activity whose ancillary effects have been shown to not only protect, but promote and (dare we say) actually facilitate business activities. Herein lies a problem: once we establish a function of close protection, what do we do to sustain it?

Beyond the tactical, there are several factors at play here:

- **Strategy.** This is the issue with many programs, which are started but fizzle out over a period of time. Started (as discussed above) based on an issue or risk, once the incident has passed, the function loses fidelity quickly. Then, as a result, the original strategy is reduced to a point at which it offers no value and cannot perform the function it was initially started for. The main reason for this is a lack of long-term strategy. Tactically, we are able to spin up the function, put in place the individual(s), perform protective intelligence, and thus create an apparatus to do the job. However, due to the lack of forethought, we don't consider the "what next" or sustaining efforts required to maintain the program after the threat or the perception of risk has passed.

- **Planning.** Along with vision, a close protective program needs the ability to map and manage the system. At some level, understanding financial controls and decision-making processes goes hand-in-hand with detail management and advance work.

- **Communications.** Being able to speak to a principal while on a detail is one thing; being able to communicate plans, strategies, and the long-term benefits of a well-thought-out protective operation is something completely different. Leaders within the protective space need to understand not only the nuances of putting together a security detail, but also the language of finance, risk mitigation and program management to effectively be able to parlay to senior leadership.

What *Corporate Executive Protection: An Introduction for Corporations and Security Professionals* aims to do is help get practitioners on the right path and help existing programs mature to the next level.

In Part I, the authors lay foundations on how to determine whether members of the leadership teams need executive protection and, if so, how protection specialists should communicate with company stakeholders. They also discuss the "how to" in creating a corporate executive protection strategy, and several practical tips such as writing effective requests for proposals (RFPs) for protective services.

You should walk away from Part I with the ability to ask the right kinds of questions about a program and to distinguish between good and bad answers concerning the "why" of a corporate executive protection program.

Part II gets a little more operational, as experience and lessons learned are shared from the authors' points of view in managing and maintaining a protection program. Growing and maintaining a program is very much a people business. The insights offered on both hard and soft skills will be helpful to both protection managers and anyone else who hopes to make a career in this amazing field.

Lastly, Part III takes a hard look at transitions. Specifically, how do you start a new executive protection program, or how do you perform turnaround within a program that's flagging? The authors again offer insight into looking for trouble signs and how to perform realignment or sustain a program that's already doing well.

What you will find here is a bounty of information that will be beneficial to everyone from the individual contributor to the corporate security manager. It's not only good as a guide to get started, it's also an important contribution to the professionalization of the industry as we move away from traditional systems and evolve with the same speed and innovation as those we are charged to protect.

Preface

Ray O'Hara, CPP
Executive Vice President, AS Solution
Former President and Chairman of the Board,
ASIS International

Corporate executive protection has come a long way in the last 10-15 years. Corporations are becoming savvier about the different kinds of security they need. Providers are becoming more professional, specialized and global in meeting those needs. And the principals—the people we serve directly—are better protected now than ever before in spite of an ever-changing range of risks and threats.

Christian West and Brian Jantzen have been at the forefront of innovation in the corporate executive protection industry for many years. I can ensure readers that they know their stuff when it comes to best practices in close protection. They also know their way around the C-suite of many major companies, and how to talk to everyone from the CEO to the executive assistant. It is this combination of hard and soft skills that has given them success in this niche industry. And it is precisely this combination of hard-nosed security know-how and corporate insight that makes their book worth reading for anyone involved in executive protection in the business world—whether you're buying or providing these services.

The first of its kind, *Corporate Executive Protection: An Introduction for Corporations and Security Professionals* gives an excellent overview of how the rubber meets the road in the real world. Christian and Brian provide insight that few others are capable of. They've been around the block more than once in every phase of a corporate executive protection program and it shows.

I believe this book will be helpful to a lot of people, and that it comes at the right time. What used to be a highly fragmented marketplace is now consolidating. Sure, there are still plenty of Mom and Pop operations that make a decent living with just a few main clients, but these are not the kind of supplier that large corporations or their principals will continue to count on. Increasingly, corporations need protective services that are reliable, scalable and global. They will want to work with specialist partners who can meet those needs.

Corporations that previously used the "I know a guy" method to find a retired law enforcement officer or military vet to handle close protection are getting smarter. They're asking tougher questions. They're looking for quality protection and value for money. This book should help them find both.

This guide is also an important contribution to the professionalization of the executive protection industry—something it sorely needs. A background in law enforcement or the military, on its own, is not enough to qualify people to work in executive protection. We need better standards for training and certifications. We need to improve HR management and provide the best and the brightest in the field with career paths and planning. We all need to get better at understanding what best-in-class protection is, and how to make it happen.

With this book, Christian and Brian take a significant step forward on behalf of all of us in the industry.

Contents

Introduction:
Why every corporation should have a proactive executive protection strategy

We're often asked why corporations establish executive protection programs for their CEOs and other employees. The question is fair enough, since corporate executive protection is a relatively new phenomenon for many companies, and by its very nature not something that people outside the boardroom, C-suite or our industry discuss much in public.

But the more we think about an answer, the more we're convinced that the question should be turned on its head. A better question is "Why wouldn't corporations establish executive protection programs for their CEOs and other C-level employees?"

1

First, let's try to understand why more and more Fortune 500 companies are setting up executive protection programs—and why every corporation really should at least consider these six reasons to write a proactive executive protection strategy.

1. You already have an executive protection strategy: Make it proactive rather than reactive

It is interesting to note that while few corporations would admit to not having a marketing or HR strategy, many of these same corporations have never thought about formulating a corporate executive protection strategy.

Whether it's implicit or explicit, however, every corporation already has an executive protection strategy. The difference is that smart companies base their strategies on a proactive process of risk analysis and mitigation, corporate culture and personal preferences. Others are more laissez-faire and reactive, employing a wait-and-see strategy that only changes when circumstances demand it.

Proactive protection programs are grounded on risk analysis and mitigation of risk to acceptable levels. First, the full spectrum of threats and vulnerabilities needs to be understood. Then, it's important to assess the impact of the risks, or losses, that the corporation would suffer should these threats actually breach vulnerabilities. Then and only then can measures be taken to mitigate risks so those rated as unacceptably high are reduced, and those rated as acceptable are tolerated for a reason.

Good corporate executive protection programs are also grounded in the company culture and the personal preferences of those to be protected. Without this grounding, the program never really takes root and becomes effective.

A corporate protection program should ideally be for all employees. After all, duty of care applies to everyone in the corporation, high and low, and the risks of doing one's job can apply at many levels. For example, a service technician traveling to a Boko Haram-controlled area of Nigeria is clearly exposed to tangible threats. So is a highly prominent CEO speaking at a public event in New York.

As we'll see below, however, there are a number of reasons why more comprehensive versions of this service are usually reserved for members of the C-suite.

2. Executive protection safeguards shareholder investment in C-level personnel

For some CEO positions, board-mandated executive protection programs come with the territory. Or should.

The CEO's prominence is one factor that plays into this, as a highly prominent business leader is more at risk from "persons of interest" precisely due to his or her notoriety. CEOs are often in the news nationally and internationally for one reason or another. They might work in an industry that is in the public spotlight or is controversial, or their personal success and details of their wealth might be the stuff of financial and gossip magazines.

As public figures, many people recognize CEOs and are fascinated by them, by how they live, and even by their families. Persons of interest might have a grudge, they might be in love, or they might be looking for a handout since their own income is considerably lower than the CEO's. They could also be potential kidnappers. In any case, risk analyses often show that the potential threats to a highly prominent CEO can be equal to or greater than those of other "celebrities" with whom they would never otherwise compare themselves.

But boards also consider the business and investor impact of an accident occurring to the CEO. As has been amply demonstrated by a number of unfortunate incidents, corporate reputations and share prices can be closely linked to an individual CEO's well-being.

When shareholder value can rise or fall dramatically with the safety of a CEO, it's natural that boards choose to safeguard their investment in the CEO with protection programs that cost a fraction of the overall compensation package.

3. Executive protection enables higher productivity of the highest paid

There's a reason the CEO has a personal assistant, travels by company jet or in business class, and doesn't have to write up the minutes of every meeting he or she participates in: productivity. The CEO is usually the highest-paid person not only in the room, but in the company.

Executive protection, in addition to keeping people safe, also enables higher productivity by making travel and everyday logistics as smooth as possible.

Secure travel eliminates waiting for cabs and standing at the car rental counter. Unlike a ride with a chatty (and often unvetted and potentially dangerous) limo driver, it also minimizes interruptions, turns travel time into work time, and lets high-paid execs pack more meetings in more places into less time than most other people can even dream of.

4. Executive protection enables more, safer travel

One of our clients once said something that has stuck with us ever since: "You guys make it easier to travel, so we travel more."

It's really as simple as that.

The CEO is typically the corporation's best salesman, evangelist and negotiator all rolled into one. Executive protection takes a lot of the friction and hassle out of traveling. So the CEO gets more face time with customers, employees, government officials and other key stakeholders worldwide.

5. Duty of care

According to law.com, duty of care is defined as follows:

> A requirement that a person act toward others and the pub-
> lic with the watchfulness, attention, caution and prudence
> that a reasonable person in the circumstances would use. If
> a person's actions do not meet this standard of care, then
> the acts are considered negligent, and any damages result-
> ing may be claimed in a lawsuit for negligence.

To paraphrase concerning corporate executive protection:

> Given the circumstances (prominence, threat levels, risk
> analyses, etc.) of their CEOs and other employees, many
> boards find it prudent and reasonable to meet a certain
> standard of care (executive protection in certain situations;
> comparisons to other similar corporations) in order to do
> the right thing and not be considered negligent.

6. Executive protection can provide a competitive advantage

Everything else being equal, if one corporation's C-level executives are more productive and safer than another's, that's a
competitive boost.

What board wouldn't want its CEO to be safer and more productive? And maybe even happier, because he or she can enjoy
the benefits of a well-conceived executive protection strategy?

Part I:
Foundations of corporate executive protection

Introduction to Part I

In the first part of our book we explore the foundations of corporate executive protection.

We open with what we think is the natural place to start: the purpose of corporate executive protection. Chapter 1 argues that in order to be truly successful, programs must do more than keep the principal safe—they must also keep the principal productive and happy as well.

In fact, some of our principals have told us that the real advantage of executive protection programs is enhanced productivity. Executive protection, when it is done right, enables the principal to get more done, travel more efficiently and make better use of time. Seen from the principal's point of view, executive protection is a productivity enabler with the side benefit of keeping him or her safe.

We are furthermore convinced that the "happiness" factor—or at least satisfaction with the program—is an important part of the equation. For unless the program adapts to the principal's corporate culture and personal preferences to meet or exceed expectations—*and* delivers seamlessly on safety and productivity—the principal will ultimately not be satisfied with the program and will want to stop it.

Chapters 2 and 3 dig into other reasons that motivate corporations to set up an executive protection program. Understanding the actual risks, threats and vulnerabilities facing a high-profile principal is an important first step. Deciding on how to mitigate these risks to an acceptable level—and designing and implementing a program to do so—is the nuts and bolts of executive protection.

Before deciding on what type of corporate executive protection program is the right one, it is important for boards to consider their options and ask some basic questions. Which executive protection services are relevant for the corporation? To what extent, when and where are these services applicable? How should they be provided? Chapter 3 provides an overview of the elements of a board-mandated corporate executive protection program based on current best practice. It also considers the differences between minimally viable and best-practice solutions.

In Chapter 4 we look at the corporate executive protection ecosystem. To be successful, corporate executive protection must mesh smoothly with many different people and parts of the organization—not only with the principal.

It is critical that executive protection managers and agents understand the roles of the many different corporate stakeholders that surround the principal and keep the organization moving; it is just as critical that these many stakeholders understand what executive protection is all about. Good communication between all is one of the things that sets good executive protection programs apart from failures.

Chapter 5 provides a rough template for writing a corporate executive protection strategy. While it does not purport to be an actual strategy, of course, is does outline the contours of a strategy process that we have used many times with our clients.

In Chapter 6 we enter the nebulous zone of governance and corporate executive protection. While there are few countries or states that actually have specific laws on their books legislating executive protection programs and activities, we hope this chapter will help those responsible for corporate executive protection programs to get a better idea of how to understand regulations, standards, policies and procedures—and their operational applications in corporate executive protection programs.

Next come some thoughts on why corporations typically decide to outsource all or part of their executive protection programs rather than build the entire function on their own. As a provider of outsourced executive protection services ourselves, we realize that we run the risk that Chapter 7 might at first glance be mere marketing. We hope that the reader will look beyond this and consider some of the points that we raise in this chapter; in our experience, keeping the principal consistently safe, happy and productive is usually more successful when at least parts of the programs are outsourced to specialist partners. To that end, Chapter 8 provides concrete advice for writing a request for proposal (RFP) for corporate executive protection services.

Chapter 1:
The Why of corporate executive protection—safe, happy and productive

Corporate executive protection is a lot of things to a lot of people. That's natural, as executive protection is a relatively new discipline in the corporate sphere. But it doesn't mean that everything that everyone says about corporate executive protection makes sense or is helpful.

That is why we are writing this book about building and maintaining a corporate executive protection program. We have had the privilege of helping some highly successful corporations set up or turn around their executive protection programs, and we've learned a few things along the way that we want to share.

"People don't buy what you do, they buy why you do it."

If you're like a lot of other people, you've already heard the above quote. It's by Simon Sinek, whose popular Ted Talk on the reasons businesses should focus on answering "Why?" rather than just "What?" or "How?" has been viewed more than 19 million times. For Sinek, having a clear understanding of the business's purpose—what we believe in—makes all the difference in the world. It's what makes us get out of bed in the morning. It's what separates great companies and leaders from the merely good. And it's what keeps customers coming back for more.

Corporate executive protection programs, in our opinion, should also be built around a simple but purposeful belief. Here is what makes us tick: We exist to keep our principals safe, happy and productive. If we get this right, the "why" of corporate executive protection, then we are off to a good start in dealing with all the "whats" and "hows." But that's the stuff of later chapters. Let's begin by looking into our "why."

First, keep the principal *safe*

Broadly defined, safety can be described as being protected from danger, risk or injury. In the executive protection world, we often talk about protection from threats, risks and vulnerabilities.

In the real world, however, not even the best politician, priest or army can ensure that anyone will always be completely safe. Guaranteed safety is just not part of the human condition. So while we executive protection professionals cannot eliminate risk, we must do everything we can to mitigate it.

Risk mitigation begins with understanding the situations that expose our principals to potential danger. We then systematically proceed to reduce the extent of our principals' exposure to these situations, as well as develop contingency procedures for dealing with the effects of breached safety to reduce their impact.

For many corporate principals, risk mitigation is equally important wherever there is exposure to risk. This could be while they are at home, at the office or on the road; the executive protection program must deal with each situation accordingly.

As in many other aspects of corporate life, risk mitigation has to do with best practices, consistency and key performance indicators (KPIs). We'll be looking more closely at all of these in later chapters.

Then, keep the principal happy

We can't think of a corporate function that gets more up close and personal with the principal (and his or her family) than executive protection. It's in the nature of the job to be near in all kinds of situations, both public and private. It can last for days at a time. It can and does get personal.

Getting the interpersonal part of the job right means more than feeling good, however. It can mean the difference between program success and failure, and thus impact the principal's safety as well as productivity.

While successful executive protection obviously cannot claim to make all principals truly happy, poorly managed programs have a good chance of making everyone a little more miserable. Good programs blend naturally into the corporation's organization and culture. In addition to maintaining consistent adherence to best practice, they are flexibly individualized to adjust to the principal's lifestyle and values.

Ultimately, however, keeping the principal happy with the executive protection program has a very simple goal: if the principal is not happy with the services rendered, or how the people involved are delivering them, then the principal will want to stop the program. No executive protection program means reduced safety and productivity.

And always keep the principal productive

When most people look at the ROI of executive administrative assistants, it is clear that the incremental costs of hiring one or more professionals can easily be offset by productivity boosts at the C-level.

Similarly, the logistical support provided by executive protection professionals allows principals to stay focused on their work and goals, and to stay productive no matter where their work takes them.

In our experience, executive protection is not a distraction when it is done properly. But it can hamper productivity rather than enhance it if it is not done professionally. The most successful executive protection programs are firmly anchored in the principal's corporate and private ecosystems. Such programs are not only the most efficient in terms of "protection per dollar"; they are also the most hassle-free and likely to keep the principal happy and safe in the long run.

Good corporate executive protection starts with keeping the principal safe, but it doesn't end there. If the purpose of your executive protection program doesn't include keeping the principal productive and happy, then we think its chances of success, in the long run, are limited.

Chapter 2:
Does your company need an executive protection program?

The decision to set up a corporate executive protection program is not a simple one. While good programs share many similarities across a variety of companies, the paths leading to the decision to establish them are as varied as the companies themselves.

Why companies choose to set up executive protection programs: To mitigate assessed risks

There are a number of factors that influence whether a corporation decides to provide a special degree of protection for some of its principals. In essence, however, all of these factors have to do with the three basic questions of risk assessment and mitigation:

- What would be the impact, or loss, if something occurred to one or more of the company's principals?

- What is the probability of that loss occurring?

- How can we best mitigate the risk?

Risk assessment and mitigation are the foundation of every executive protection program, and should inform all corporate executive protection strategies. While a "how to" of risk assessment is beyond the scope of this book, we will take a quick look at each of the three central questions—and return to more risk assessment details later.

Impact of loss

The potential losses related to a corporate principal being harmed are many and varied. Obviously, the most important are the personal consequences of any harm to the individual and his or her family.

Beyond that, however, lie other interests of the company and its shareholders. That is why the corporation's board of directors typically considers a spectrum of factors when deciding whether to mandate an executive protection program for one or more of its principals.

One factor is shareholder value. If a corporation's reputation and competitiveness are closely associated with one or two high-profile individuals, then the company's perceived value—and actual share price—can be immediately affected if something happens to those individuals.

Duty of care is another issue. If individuals working for the corporation are exposed to personal risk as part of their jobs, then executive protection may in some cases be considered a duty of care since it could mitigate a reasonable and foreseeable risk.

Another potential "loss," which is often overlooked, has to do with productivity. Few boards would expect a well-remunerated top executive to spend time making his or her own travel arrangements. But what about the time execs spend moving between airports, hotels and meetings while traveling? Secure travel logistics, a key component of many executive protection programs, not only keeps executives safer while on the road, it also enables them to boost productivity by staying focused on the job rather than dealing with rental cars and taxi queues.

It is impossible to make blanket statements about the possible impact on a corporation should something occur to some of its principals: there are just too many variables that need to be considered. A detailed risk analysis can, however, make things more clear for boards and management—and should be a part of every executive protection strategy.

Probability of risk

The assessment of risk probability for a corporate principal is affected by a number of factors.

Specific threats from persons of interest to the principal or his or her family are typically at the top of the list, and need to be perceived and analyzed to keep people safe now and in future. Understandably, such threats are often a part of the company's decision to instigate an executive protection program. However, we know from experience—and from the Secret Service's "Exceptional Case Study Project"—that those who pose the biggest threats are rarely those who actually make direct threats. This means that assessing risk probability entails more than recording actual threats; it should also encompass proactive intelligence to identify probable and possible persons and groups of interest.

For reasons that include everything from crime and income inequality to terrorism and road traffic, risk is perceived to be greater in some cities and countries than in others. An investment banker traveling to Bogotá is more at risk than one traveling to Boston. And while we're on the topic of travel, do you know what the biggest single risk while traveling is? Getting hurt in a road accident while driving in a car.

Another key indicator of risk probability is prominence. The more prominent a corporation and its principals, the more likely they are to be approached by persons of interest. These interactions range from slight to enormous invasions of privacy; they include troublesome but largely innocuous exchanges with strangers (you're rich, I'm not—how about giving me some of your money?); they can also be outright hostile (kidnapping of the principal or his family). There are tools to evaluate the relative prominence of various principals, and these should be used in assessing the probability of risk.

Everything else being equal, furthermore, some industries are more prominent than others. This, too should be taken into consideration when assessing risk. For example, the oil and gas industry is under close scrutiny from many quarters, not all of them friendly. The number of persons, disaffected or otherwise, who take an interest in a petroleum company and its principals is likely to be higher than those who keep an eye on a food company. Until someone has a beef with the food company's products, that is.

Mitigating risk

Risk mitigation is not the same as risk elimination. Like everything else that has to do with risk assessment, there are no absolutes that hold true for mitigating risk.

Yes, we would dramatically reduce risk to the principal if we required him or her never to travel and to remain ensconced in a fortress of a corporate headquarters. But is this realistic?

Conversely, mustering a formidable force to accompany execs on their travels would allow safe mobility but is not an attractive option. For most companies, setting up the equivalent of the U.S. Marines to protect key principals is neither desirable nor feasible.

Mitigating risk is what executive protection is all about. It is a question of striking the right balance between many factors. To mention a few: the relative probability of perceived and possible threats, the principal's lifestyle and travel needs, corporate organization and culture, available resources and budgets.

The "how" of risk mitigation is the "who, what, when, where and how" of executive protection. Who should be protected, and by whom? What are the elements of that protection? When, where and how should protection take place? How should an executive protection program be organized, managed and evaluated? These are all questions that need to be answered in a corporate executive protection strategy.

Toward a corporate executive protection strategy

We conclude this chapter by returning to our original question. Does your company need an executive protection program? Sorry, but we believe there is no straightforward answer. Every corporate security officer—and ultimately every corporate board of directors—needs to consider this in light of their executive protection strategy.

Because whether it is written down or not, every company does have a corporate executive protection strategy.

Some corporations simply figure that the chances of anything happening to their principals are negligible, and that they'd easily be able to deal with the loss of a principal if something did happen. That is also a strategy.

Corporate decision makers should take the time to learn about the many ways that executive protection programs can be customized to fit the company's specific needs. Otherwise, they risk adopting a generic or outdated strategy based on inaccurate assumptions—and results can be more frustrating than they are effective.

Those companies that do make the effort to proactively create a corporate executive protection strategy take a different approach. First, they make an active decision to face the three basic questions of risk assessment and mitigation outlined above. Then, they consider their options and choose the path that best suits them.

In our experience, few corporations—including even large, international ones—have faced all of the questions we discuss above in a coherent way; even fewer have created a corporate executive protection strategy. Even though corporate executive protection is growing, both in terms of the number of companies using it in one way or another and in professionalism, in most companies it has yet to reach anywhere near the levels of expertise found in other corporate functions such as finance, HR, sales or marketing. (None of which, by the way, would dream of operating without a strategy!)

Chapter 3:
The five questions board members must ask before mandating a corporate executive protection program

When it comes to corporate executive protection, no two companies are alike. Every corporation has different needs, cultures, locations and, not least, principals with their own requirements and preferences.

But while there is nothing "one size fits all" about corporate executive protection implementation, the questions that a board asks before mandating a corporate executive protection program should be basically the same every time.

We say "should be" because, in our experience, they often aren't. Too many companies jump, slide or limp into an executive protection program without first considering all their options. Instead, they should ask at least five questions.

Who is to be protected?

The number of protected persons will depend on the outcome of the initial Risk, Threat and Vulnerability Assessment (RTVA), but will typically start with one or more corporate executives.

Executive protection programs can scale from there. Depending on circumstances, protection may be extended to additional corporate principals as well as spouses or children.

When are they to be protected?

Some executive protection programs begin on an ad hoc basis, for example with travel to high-risk areas. Some are only for work-related travels and activities. Still others are designed for true 7/24/365 coverage, no matter where the principal's work or other interests take him or her. Whether your executive protection program is designed to provide comprehensive, round-the-clock protection or more limited security should depend on the outcome of the RTVA and the resultant program objectives.

Minimally viable programs start with the highest-risk circumstances. Interestingly, the most frequent cause of injury is far less spectacular than terrorist attacks: traffic accidents are the single most likely cause of harm for most travelers, so well-planned executive protection programs often start with secure transportation during travel to selected territories.

What kinds of protection are necessary?

Modern executive protection is enabled by a combination of

human resources and technology. An effective, industry-standard executive protection program is a system that integrates most—and ideally all—of seven building blocks:

1. Alarm monitoring, access control and trained security agents for controlling access to the principal's workplace and residence.

2. Security drivers trained in executive protection and defensive/evasive driving.

3. Automobile(s) specially equipped for security.

4. Flights on charter aircraft for business and personal purposes.

5. Close personal protection provided by trained and carefully selected executive protection agents at home, at work or while traveling.

6. Intelligence analysts that monitor, investigate and report on people of interest, inappropriate communications and threats, and also provide risk analysis and travel risk assessments for the employee's scheduled trips and events.

7. Surveillance and antisurveillance that identifies and deters potential attackers before an attack.

Minimally viable executive protection programs typically include some combination of the first four elements. This combination of access control and secure transportation can be considered the "baby steps" of corporate executive protection, and this is the right way to begin.

Best-practice executive protection programs include elements five and six—usually at the same time and in an integrated fashion to maximize the protective effect and make best use of executive protection manpower resources. Depending on the scale of the operation, the same group of executive protection agents can provide both close protection and intel—at least initially.

The seventh element, which includes the integration of surveillance and anti-surveillance services, is typically reserved for either very-high-profile individuals and their families or situations of elevated threat level.

Where should they be protected?

Just where the employee should be protected is a key question that every executive protection strategy must answer. As principals move through their working and personal lives, they travel through a wide variety of locations, each with its particular advantages and disadvantages from a security point of view.

Best-in-class executive protection programs must be ready to function wherever the principals' lifestyles take them. Minimally viable programs will focus on those locations that represent the highest risks, and mitigate those. Whether or not—and to what extent—the program will include all conceivable locations should depend on the risk analysis and executive protection strategy. Places to consider include:

At the principal's residence

The principal's residence should be covered by both an alarm and a video system that are monitored 24x7x365 at a dedicated central station either on the property or remotely.

In addition to this electronic surveillance, protection agents can be deployed in a number of ways. Some of these options, listed below in order of increasing effectiveness, are:

- **Option 1:** Contract with a third-party security provider to monitor residential alarm and video systems and respond if needed.

- **Option 2:** One or several security agents provide coverage from vehicles parked outside the property. With access to alarms and video feeds, they provide a deterrent and can respond to privacy or security threats. The agents are connected to a remote Security Operations Center (SOC) for communication, reporting and support.

- **Option 3:** Two agents provide coverage from within the property. Working in shifts 24x7x365, one agent monitors alarms and video feeds, and the other provides response. The SOC is a room on the property with its own facilities for the security agents so coverage is continuous despite restroom or meal breaks.

- **Option 4:** Add protective surveillance and anti-surveillance teams to Option 3 in order to monitor movements outside the property.

During commute to and from work

The predictability of the times and locations involved with commuting between home and work increases the risk of attack or harassment. Security professionals can mitigate these risks.

Again, there are a number of options regarding how to protect employees during their daily commutes. Some of these are listed below, but the one that is right for your program will depend on the outcome of a reliable executive protection contractor's analysis and recommendations. Among other criteria, choosing the best option relies on an understanding of risk and risk tolerance and on the principal's personal preferences.

- **Option 1:** Provide a vehicle with a trained security driver to the employee for his or her commute to and from work. The driver should be trained in surveillance detection, evasive/defensive driving, vehicle dynamics and executive protection. The driver should also have the driving skills of a chauffeur to provide a high level of comfort and service to the employee. An added benefit of this option is that the employee can stay productive during the commute instead of driving.

- **Option 2:** If the employee prefers to drive himself or herself, provide a surveillance vehicle for each transfer. This requires a dedicated, discreet security vehicle and two highly trained security agents so that one can effectively drive the vehicle while the second is alert to the environments around the employee's vehicle during transit. It also provides a more effective response resource to handle issues and threats to the employee.

At work

One or more executive protection agents can be assigned to stay in the vicinity of the employee while at work. These executive protection agents are tasked with immediate response in case of any issues or threats. An additional executive protection agent should man the corporate SOC to monitor alarms and video.

While traveling

An effective travel protection program includes advance work, redundancy of resources and, of course, proper talent selection. Best-practice travel protection support typically includes:

- Two executive protection agents—one for advance work and one for close-in protection. The two executive protection agents should travel to the destination(s) in advance of the employee's arrival with enough time to prepare both security and logistics plans using industry best practices/advance work techniques. They also ensure the quality and appropriateness of all drivers and vehicles. For higher-risk or more complex destinations, vetted and reliable contracted executive protection resources should be utilized at the destination(s) for additional team support.

- A primary vehicle and security trained driver for transporting the employee and others in his or her party.

- A backup vehicle and security trained driver to be used for additional group members and as a quick replacement for the primary vehicle in case the primary becomes unavailable for any reason (mechanical issues, road traffic accident, etc.).

- An advance vehicle and security trained driver that is used by the advance agent to move ahead of the employee (30–60 minutes) to ensure that the next destination is safe and properly prepared for an efficient and appropriate arrival.

Two of the many considerations applicable here are whether such protection should be provided whenever the employee is outside his or her home or office, or only for work-related travel.

At public or semi-public events

If the principal is required to participate in corporate or other events that are open to the public—say, an annual shareholders' meeting—then it is important that the security around such participation is adequate.

While close personal protection of the principal would be an expected part of the executive protection program, dedicated event security procedures might also be relevant both to safeguard all employees and shareholders and to protect the corporation's overall interests from threats.

At other family members' activities

If the executive protection program includes other family members in addition to the employee, then those individuals will also require close personal protection wherever their schedules and lifestyles take them.

This can include school and extracurricular activities for children, work and leisure activities for spouses, etc.

What's the difference between "good enough," common and best-practice corporate executive protection?

Corporate boards that are not experienced in executive protection—and few are—often have a difficult time determining the level of protection that they should provide for a principal.

Unlike other issues on the agenda at board meetings, the distinctions between common and best practice regarding executive protection programs may seem unclear and unproven to board members. Whereas few boards would doubt what distinguishes unacceptable, good and great financial reporting, for example, even fewer are likely to have an informed opinion about the elements of a best-in-class executive protection solution—let alone a minimally viable executive protection program.

Given this lack of expertise in an area that is, put bluntly, of life and death importance to the corporation's key principals or even its market value, it's no wonder that many boards have a difficult time deciding whether or not to mandate a corporate executive protection program.

The resulting situation and level of executive protection provided for selected principals is thus not the result of a proactive decision-making process, but is often determined by inertia or reactions to sudden threat scenarios.

We believe that it is not only possible, but indeed essential, to build corporate executive protection programs that scale from the minimally viable to the more complex. It is a good idea to begin with baby steps, and corporations should begin with "must-have" essentials before they move to "nice-to-have" add-ons. And they should regularly review their programs to make sure that they are "just right."

Just how any individual corporation should do this will depend on an up-to-date risk assessment and the resultant executive protection strategy. It will also depend on whether the corporation is starting up a new executive protection program, maintaining one that works, or turning around an executive protection program that has run into difficulties.

Given the specialized nature of corporate executive protection and most board members' lack of experience in designing effective executive protection programs, it is highly recommended that the board cooperate with a reputable executive protection contractor to help determine the right level of protection.

A good executive protection program is more than the sum of its parts

Now that we've lined up the elements of a good executive protection program, let's be clear about one more thing: A corporate executive protection program is about much more than choosing from a catalog of elements.

In our experience, the success of corporate executive protection also depends on:

- An effective understanding of how the executive protection program integrates with the rest of the corporate organization,

- Knowledge of and respect for the principal's lifestyle and personal preferences as regards executive protection,

- An intelligent and thorough executive protection strategy and

- Well-trained, carefully selected executive protection staff.

But that's the stuff of future chapters.

Chapter 4:
The corporate executive protection ecosystem

The difference between corporate executive protection and executive protection in other contexts is, well, corporate. When executive protection takes place in the context of the modern corporation it must play by a very different set of rules than close protection of political or military VIPs and celebrities. Corporate executive protection managers need to navigate between many interests—often conflicting. The single most important thing is getting the culture right.

Culture eats strategy for breakfast

Executive protection managers at major corporations would do well to remember the words of management guru Peter Drucker: "Company cultures are like country cultures. Never try to change one. Try, instead, to work with what you've got."

Because no matter what an executive protection manager may have learned in the military or law enforcement, working in a modern corporation is different in so many ways. Let's examine a few of them:

- **Structure:** Vertical hierarchies are replaced by the matrix organization, where one person may have multiple reporting lines and loyalties, and conflicts of interest are common.

- **Rules of conduct:** Proper behavior is more implied or understood than defined by explicit rules.

- **Rank and status:** While rank is clearly marked and understood in the military, those with influence in corporations are not always identifiable by their titles.

- **Career progression:** Unlike the military's clear career ladder, corporate employees have a more varied career flow. Lateral job changes in a matrix organization can bring significant changes to one's career.

If a corporate executive protection manager and agents are going to have success, then they need to understand that corporate cultures all vary, and that no two corporations are alike.

For one thing, there are significant differences between industries. Just look at how cultures in tech start-ups differ from pharmaceutical or oil and gas companies. But there are significant differences within the same industries, too. To thrive, executive protection professionals must have an excellent understanding of the corporation's mission, values, beliefs, power structures, stories...and everything else that underpins corporate culture.

Navigating the organizational chart: Know your stakeholders

Corporate executive protection managers are typically tasked with protecting one or more C-level principals. But this does not mean that the principal is the only individual with whom they need to develop working relationships.

To the contrary, successful executive protection managers need to know all of the many stakeholders in corporate executive protection, and establish strong collaborative relationships throughout the ecosystem. Most stakeholder analyses will include the following persons and departments—or their equivalents.

Executive administrative assistants to the principal

The executive administrative assistant (EAA) to the principal is your most important stakeholder in the entire organization. Bar none. The EAA is your gateway to the principal—and also the gatekeeper who stands between you and the principal.

The EAA has all the information on the principal's meeting and travel schedules. This is the bread and butter information that enables the executive protection team to do advance, operative and team planning and get their job done. As schedules often change—sometimes at the last minute—having an open line to the EAA is essential.

The EAA is the main communication channel between the executive protection manager and the principal. Not only does the EAA keep you informed of the principal's comings and goings, but he or she is also the one who is most likely to get direct feedback from the principal about the executive protection team, and then send it on to you. For example, the EAA might know that the principal was unhappy with an agent's behavior before the executive protection manager or the agent does. You want to be the next one to know—not the last—so you can take action.

But the EAA also plays another important role in corporate executive protection. She or he can be your greatest ally in helping the principal understand what the executive protection team does and why it needs to do what it does. The EAA can also help others in the organization comprehend how executive protection agents do their jobs. The EAA's understanding of executive protection is invaluable. For example, knowing that the executive protection team needs to conduct advance work for trips allows the EAA to plan trip itineraries accordingly. Sometimes a little understanding goes a long way in smoothing out the inevitable frictions that arise in a fast-paced corporate environment.

Partnership between the executive protection team and the EAA is essential given the many interdependencies between the two. It allows both parties to do their jobs well, and it is a two-way street.

For example, the executive protection team often functions as an extension of the EAA's office when the principal is on the road. Let's say the principal is traveling abroad and needs a presentation that a team back at HQ is working on up until the last minute before an important meeting in a hotel. The EAA can depend on the executive protection team to get the file by secure email, get it printed and get it into the principal's hands within minutes; after all, the executive protection team knows the layout of the hotel and can make arrangements with the business center—all while maintaining security and confidentiality.

Never make the EAA say "I don't know" to the principal. Keep her or him informed of what you're doing, why you're doing it, who's on the team—and who's got the ball on all the important tasks.

Corporate communications/public relations

Executive protection teams need to understand what corporate communications/public relations (PR) teams do, and vice versa. And they need an open and ongoing dialogue. Both parties have an interest in many of the same things, albeit often for different reasons.

To some extent, we're both concerned with prominence. Public relations (PR) professionals are tasked with building and maintaining corporate reputations as well as those of their key principals. Media prominence for the right things is an important goal for, and result of, their work.

For executive protection professionals, however, "increased prominence" often translates into "increased risk."

We need to know about any plans and activities by corporate communications that can predictably increase our principal's prominence. Controversial topics can quickly turn into hot buttons for everyone from activists to anarchists. Rightly or wrongly, the principal immediately becomes the lightning rod for all kinds of people with all kinds of grief, and folks with an axe to grind might end up wielding the axe. Executive protection managers need to know what might bump up a principal's prominence prior to any major announcement so that they can plan accordingly.

The executive protection team needs to learn from corporate communications how to handle the press. We never want to be part of the story, but we should be able to help journalists get theirs when possible and in accordance with a coordinated plan developed by the PR and executive protection teams together.

Proper training and coordination enables frontline executive protection agents to redirect press away from a principal and toward the appropriate contact. The result enhances security for the principal and gives journalists access to someone who can provide the information they're looking for.

Corporate travel

Executive protection managers should maintain good relationships with the corporate travel department.

We have to move with the principal, frequently at short notice, and corporate travel employees are often the people who help us with air travel, short-notice visa applications, hotels and many other practicalities.

Travel departments may have to bend corporate procedures to enable executive protection agents to do their jobs. If the principal is staying at the Four Seasons, then some of the executive protection team will also have to stay at the Four Seasons, even though the price exceeds normal guidelines.

Executive protection agents who maintain good relationships with their counterparts in corporate travel are happy executive protection agents. It's not hard to do if you remember some of the things your mother tried to teach you: be nice, treat people with respect, say please and thank you. And remember to apologize when you have to make them jump through hoops for you.

Legal

The executive protection team needs to consult with the legal department for a number of reasons.

Use-of-force policies and practices must always be cleared with legal in order to mitigate the risk of litigation.

People of interest must be handled in a coordinated partnership, so that the executive protection team (with the possible support of intelligence analysts) takes care of personal security, and legal takes care of relations with law enforcement if restraining orders are needed. If such a threat goes public, then corporate communications will also be part of the picture.

Finance

While executive protection may be a way of life for us in the industry, it's just another cost center for the bean counters. And a highly unpredictable one at that.

Fixed executive protection costs are not difficult to budget, but many variable costs are activity-driven. Unplanned trips happen all the time, and unexpected turns of events can easily add costs fast. We want executive protection teams to act responsibly and keep their budgets, of course, but when the security of the principal is at stake we also want them to think fast and have their priorities in order. Sticking to the budget no matter what might be responsible behavior for a marketing department, but this is not necessarily the case for corporate executive protection.

Does this mean that finance departments give executive protection teams carte blanche to run up expenses? Of course not. It does mean that executive protection managers need to keep finance informed about expenses as they develop.

Human resources (HR)

Depending on how the corporate executive protection effort is organized, corporate HR may or may not be an important interface.

If the entire executive protection program is contracted, even if some of the team are embedded within the corporation, then all HR responsibility rests on the executive protection company, not on the principal's corporation.

If, on the other hand, some or all members of the executive protection team are full-time employees of the corporation, then the executive protection manager has an important reason to talk to HR: corporate HR departments rarely have any experience with the special career paths of an executive protection manager or agent, and they need help in recruiting, understanding how to evaluate performance, establishing job ladders and career planning, and all of the other things HR operations typically handle for other departments.

If an executive protection professional employed by the company doesn't get any assistance or understanding from the corporation when it comes to a career path, the professional will have to find his or her own path. Unfortunately for the corporation, this path might lead the executive protection professional to another job in another company where career advancement opportunities are more clearly defined.

Other security-related departments and vendors

Executive protection teams will have direct liaison with a number of other corporate functions and external vendors that also form part of corporate security efforts.

In some cases, these teams will be under the same management as the executive protection team. In others, reporting lines will be different. In any case, it is important that corporate executive protection teams build and maintain close partnerships with all of the following:

- **Physical security:** As the protectors of the corporate grounds and all of its buildings, assets and staff, security officers and the rest of the physical security team play a vital role in the overall, day-to-day protection of the corporation. In terms of protecting the principal, they also play a key role. They keep persons of interest (POIs) outside of the corporate campus and far away from the principal while he or she is within the corporate perimeter. Clear communication between the executive protection and physical security teams is crucial. The physical protection team doesn't necessarily know where the principal is; the executive protection team does. Good communication between the two teams can prevent or mitigate situations in which a breach of overall physical security can affect that of the principal.

  — **Security operations center:** Both the physical protection teams and the executive protection teams might share the same hub through which they coordinate corporate and personal security.

— **Security technology resources:** Similarly, both teams will ideally have access to the same technologies (e.g., video feeds, building entrance and exit data, etc.) that enable them to do their jobs.

- **Intelligence analysts:** Analysts may or may not be an integrated part of the executive protection team. In any case, regular communication between executive protection and analysts is an important part of keeping the principal secure. Executive protection relies on intelligence to discern emerging threats and persons of interest. We also depend on intelligence for updates on countries and cities where we will be traveling with the principal, so that we can prepare and plan accordingly.

- **Family offices:** A principal will often maintain a family office to manage the family's personal financial, philanthropic or other affairs. Spouses or other family members of the principal are often involved. The executive protection team must also keep communication lines to the family office open and clear; travel and social commitments that originate within the family office must be coordinated with those of the corporation so that the executive protection team can provide seamless protection of the principal and his or her family as required.

- **Estate management:** The executive protection manager must also coordinate closely with estate managers and staff on matters like background checks for nannies and other staff and check-in processes for guests and service personnel.

- **External vendors and contractors:** Corporate executive protection managers depend on external suppliers to supplement their own teams as needs arise. For example, few corporations have the need or capacity to maintain their own vetted drivers in capitals in Latin

America, even though their principals might need to travel there occasionally. The executive protection manager relies instead on external, secure transportation providers. By working with a lead supplier for secure transportation or embedded executive protection agents, an executive protection manager can increase responsiveness and scale up or down rapidly as needs change.

Communication is key

Consistent, effective communication between the executive protection team and other parts of the corporate executive protection ecosystem is what sets successful programs apart from failures.

Put simply, it's all about doing your job and helping other people in the organization to do theirs. A good understanding of the organization helps you to engage the proper cross-organizational resources proactively rather than creating extra work and frustration. A good understanding of the executive protection effort enables others in the organization to contribute to it. Good communication helps the rest of the corporation understand the "why" of the executive protection program—keeping the principal safe, happy and productive—and motivates others to help the executive protection team.

It is the responsibility of the executive protection manager to communicate openly and clearly to other corporate stakeholders about a number of issues, including

- The purpose of the executive protection program

- The importance of an on-going Risk, Threat and Vulnerability Assessment (RTVA) mind-set as the foundation of protecting the principal

- Mutual understanding and shared views of standard executive protection operating procedures

- Operational follow-up and reporting

Regular, face-to-face meeting with key stakeholders is important. With some, such as the EAA, these meetings may be weekly. With others, they may be monthly or quarterly. Whatever the frequency, the executive protection manager needs to address all relevant issues openly.

Documentation of activities and recommendations is crucial to enable others to understand how executive protection works. Make sure that it goes upward within your chain of command and to other key stakeholders.

In a corporate setup that is not familiar with executive protection, the executive protection manager will often have to explain the value and importance of specific executive protection activities. You should back up recommendations with data and rational arguments. Rather than using military jargon or processes that you may be familiar with, frame recommendations in a way that is familiar to the corporation.

In addition to explaining executive protection to corporate stakeholders who may not be familiar with its thinking and procedures, good documentation leaves a trail that we can revisit in case something goes wrong, allowing us to learn from mistakes and continually improve on our corporate executive protection programs.

Chapter 5:
How to write a corporate executive protection strategy

So you want to write a corporate executive protection strategy, and you're looking for a template. Good luck. Because unlike many other aspects of corporate life, executive protection often seems to be implemented without a strategy.

There just aren't many corporate executive protection strategy documents lying around either in corporate headquarters or in executive protection companies. Blueprints that cover the strategy essentials are not available online. Why? We believe this is due to two simple but interrelated factors:

- Most people who know a lot about corporate strategy don't know much about executive protection.

- Most people who know a lot about executive protection don't know much about corporate strategy.

A corporate executive protection strategy template is a good start

But just because there aren't many examples to build on doesn't mean a strategic approach to corporate executive protection isn't important. Just ask any business manager, military officer or coach: A simple strategy is better than none, and a little planning goes a long way in winning both the battle and the war.

In this chapter we'd like to share a process that we go through while planning executive protection programs for our corporate clients. Let us be the first to admit it: This template is far from rocket science, and a lot of our MBA friends will certainly be able to come up with more cutting-edge corporate strategy templates.

But we're convinced that asking and answering the right questions in an orderly sequence will help everyone involved—both on the corporate and on the executive protection side of the table—to create a planning process and document that will make a huge difference.

Here is our skeleton template for corporate executive protection strategy. We'll leave it up to you to put some meat on the bones, and to answer the questions in a way that aligns best practices in both the corporate and executive protection worlds.

Introduction/summary

Feel free to write this after the rest of the plan is written. And be aware that many people won't read much more than this.

- **Statement of purpose:** In broad terms, what are your reasons for creating a corporate executive protection strategy? Why will the world, or at least your corporation, be a better place once you have written a watertight strategy?

- **Background:**

  — How do corporate values, history and business objectives relate to the executive protection strategy?

  — Are there any events, developments or other reasons that make the plan necessary now? Don't forget to consider

    ▪ Personal risks

    ▪ Business risks

    ▪ Board mandate

    ▪ Duty of care and corporate liability issues

- **Objectives:** What are you trying to achieve? Try to be as specific and measurable as possible.

  — What are the goals and **expected outcomes/results** of the executive protection program?

  — What would be the **key benefits of achieving those goals**—for the corporation and for the principal?

  — Can you boil the program down to some **simple guiding principles** that are easy for everyone to understand and remember?

- **Key success factors:** What elements of the program are critical in order for it to be successful? "If we get these parts right, we are on our way to a great program." What are the parts?

- **Key performance indicators:** Top line, what do you need to measure in order to know whether your executive protection program is on track? Consider "hard" factors like budget and schedules—as well as "soft" factors like principal satisfaction.

- **Governance**:

  — Who makes decisions about corporate executive protection?

  — Based on what criteria?

Situation analysis

This is similar to the well-known SWOT analyses so familiar to the corporate world. In the executive protection industry, we call this an RTVA. The purpose of the SWOT and the RTVA exercises is similar: Know where you stand before you start planning how to move ahead!

- Risk, Threat and Vulnerability Assessment (RTVA)

  — External factors not in our control

    ▪ Are there direct threats and security risks to the corporation or principal?

    ▪ Are there **indirect threats**, e.g., security risks not directly targeting the company or its principal(s) but present in regions where the company operates?

    ▪ What would be the **impact**, or loss, should these threats be realized?

    ▪ How **vulnerable** are we to these threats should they be realized?

  — Internal factors in our control

    ▪ What is the status/evaluation of our current executive protection and security programs?

    ▪ How do we evaluate security vulnerabilities?

- Evaluation of current and past executive protection efforts: **What lessons have we learned?**

- What parts of the **corporate ecosystem** are relevant to the executive protection effort?

- What are the **principal's personal preferences** regarding executive protection and his or her lifestyle?

- **Gap analysis:** Where are we now compared to our goals?

Executive protection program design

- **WHO** is to be protected?

  — List of principal(s)/corporate position(s) (e.g., CEO, COO, etc.) that are to be protected by the executive protection program.

  — Are any other persons related to the principals, e.g., family, also to be protected?

  — Are all persons to be provided the same level of protection? Why or why not?

- **WHEN** are the principals to be protected?

  — 24/7/365?

  — Only while traveling for the company? To all destinations or only some?

  — In other circumstances?

- **WHERE** are the principals to be protected? To all destinations or only some?

  — At home

  — At work

— While commuting home/work

— While traveling

- Abroad—high-, medium- and low-risk territories?

- Domestically

- Business

- Personal

— At corporate or other events

— At other family members' activities

- **WHAT** kinds and levels of protection are necessary?

— Alarm monitoring, access control and trained security agents for controlling access to the principal's workplace and residence

— Close personal protection provided by trained executive protection agents at home, at work or while commuting or traveling

— Security drivers trained in executive protection and defensive/evasive driving

— Automobile(s) specially equipped for security

— Intelligence analysts who monitor, investigate and report on people of interest, inappropriate communications and threats, and also provide risk analysis and travel risk assessments for the principal's scheduled trips and events

— Surveillance and anti-surveillance protection that identifies and deters potential attackers prior to any attack

— Flights on charter aircraft for business and personal reasons

Executive Protection Teams and Organization

- Draw up an organizational plan that describes the executive protection organization and its lines to other parts of the corporate organization.

- What are the key **job descriptions and qualifications**?

- How does the executive protection team **interface** with the rest of the corporate organization?

  — **Stakeholder analysis:** Who else in the organization does the executive protection team need to work with? Why is this important?

  — What are the **communication procedures** between the executive protection organization and other corporate departments?

- Training

  — Who should be trained or certified for what and to which level?

  — What are our training program and procedures?

- Career planning

  — How do we help executive protection agents and managers continue to develop their capabilities and career—so they stay with us rather than move on?

  — Alignment with corporate HR strategies and procedures?

- Program scoping

— How do we scale up or down as needs change? Which costs should be considered as fixed and which are variable?

Procurement strategy

- For technology

  — Which tech do we need?

  — How do we buy it?

  — Alignment with corporate procurement strategies?

- For human resources

  — Make/buy: Do we insource, outsource or embed key executive protection positions? Be sure to read Chapter 7 also: we have an opinion on this one!

    - The executive protection manager

    - Executive protection agents

    - Residential agents

    - Intel analysts

  — How do we search, shortlist and evaluate the executive protection companies we want to work with?

  — Are our contract management and policies in order?

Program delivery and maintenance

- What are the **Standard Operating Procedures** (SOPs) for all key processes?

- How do we **assess security risks on an ongoing basis**? How often do we update RTVAs? Do we do it ourselves, or ask for third-party assistance?

- How do we continually improve the skills of our staff?

  — Security exercises and drills: frequency, scope, post-drill evaluation, data collection....

- How do we **inspect and assess the quality** of our own security measures?

  — Internal evaluation

  — External audits

  — Red teaming

Reporting and KPI measurement

- Which **KPIs** do we follow and measure program success against? Consider both the "hard" criteria such as the well-being of the principal, budget adherence, etc., and also "soft" criteria such as the principal's satisfaction and team motivation.

- Which **reports** do we create on a regular basis? What do they contain? Who writes them? Who reads them?

- Which ad hoc reports will be necessary, when?

Budget

- What are program **setup costs**?

- What are ongoing program costs?

  — Fixed

  — Variable

- Who has budget responsibility?

- What are the procedures for financial reporting?

- What do we do about budget/actual deviations?

Implementation plan

- What are the critical path milestones for developing and implementing the executive protection program?

- Who has responsibility for moving the program forward?

- Who approves what, when?

Appendices and additional notes

- Is there extra information relevant to the strategy?

- Do we need a glossary of terms?

- References and resources

- Special circumstances

So there you have it, a tried and tested way to structure a corporate executive protection strategy. We firmly believe that time spent on developing a corporate executive protection strategy is well spent, and that even if you don't fill in all of the blanks, covering the main points will serve your program well.

Chapter 6:
Connecting the dots between regulations, standards, policies and procedures—and their operational applications in corporate executive protection

Like many other aspects of corporate life, executive protection efforts need to be managed in accordance with any applicable legislation or regulations. Solid standards must be defined and enforced. Finally, procedures based on firm policies—all consistent with standards and regulations—need to be put into place. All of this points to the need for effective governance of corporate executive protection programs.

This chapter intends to present a framework that executive protection management—as well as corporate management and even the board of directors that oversee corporate executive protection programs—can use to connect the many layers that add up to effective governance, and enable effective reporting and follow-up.

Why does your corporate executive protection program need good governance, and who needs to be involved?

Ultimate responsibility for governance of corporate executive protection lies with the board, whereas executive protection management can and should be held accountable for the policies and procedures that drive program deliverables.

Proper governance answers a range of important questions that include:

- Why do we have a corporate executive protection program?

- Are the program's structure and its operations in line with applicable legislation and company policies?

- Who is responsible for what?

- Who needs to know what about program performance metrics?

When these questions can be answered clearly and directly by executive protection management, the C-suite and the board, you are likely to be operating a well-governed executive protection program.

Executive protection legislation and regulations: A work in progress

Although it is beyond the scope of this book to provide an overview of all applicable legislation, to our knowledge there are no federal or state laws written *directly* to impact corporate executive protection. With that said, there are a number of regulatory and other legal issues which, depending on the situation and location, can affect a corporate executive protection program and its governance:

- **Licensing:** Some jurisdictions require executive protection providers to be licensed. Most do not. To be on the safe side, be sure that any individual or company involved in your executive protection program—be it a full-time employee or a third-party vendor—lives up to any applicable licensing requirements. This can include everything from the provision of bodyguard or residential security services to specialized driving skills to the use of firearms.

- **Duty of care:** This is an issue often discussed in vague terms but rarely dealt with specifically until it is too late. For the purposes of this chapter, suffice it to say that the corporation needs to be aware of how the provision of executive protection services can mitigate known risks, and thus protect the corporation against negligence suits.

- **Liability insurance:** All executive protection providers should be covered by suitable liability insurance, and those responsible for procurement should consider it their responsibility to make sure security providers have suitable coverage.

- **IRS regulations:** In the United States, the IRS may consider some executive protection services to be a taxable fringe benefit unless certain conditions are met. Fortunately, these conditions are broadly consistent with what a professionally conducted RTVA would conclude as the basis for an executive protection program. For example, IRS regulation §1.132-5(m) stipulates that security-related transportation services are not considered taxable income when they are rendered in connection with a bona fide security concern.

Setting standards for good corporate executive protection

Since you won't be able to find a set of commonly agreed standards for good corporate executive protection in any textbook, you'll have to make your own.

To our way of thinking, standards are different from policies and procedures in several ways. They should be seen as guiding principles rather than specific rules. They are value-based and not necessarily defined by simple objective criteria. They have to do with ethics, conduct and performance.

Standards are important because they set shared expectations for everyone involved in the corporate executive protection effort, including the principal and his or her organization as well as all staff and vendors involved in program deliverables. Standards are what allow us to benchmark, distinguish good performance from bad, and decide between right and wrong in case of disputes.

While every executive protection organization will ultimately have to set its own standards of excellence, here are nine guiding principles that we use. We believe that they can be helpful for others, too.

- **The principal is the priority:** That is the foundation of protection excellence. Enough said.

- **Trust:** The principal must be able to trust the executive protection team; furthermore, everyone on the team and in contact with it must be able to trust each other.

- **Consistency:** An executive protection program is as good as it is consistent. There should be one set of policies and procedures, not several. Everyone on the team should use the same approach for the principal, so there are no favorites.

- **Resourcefulness:** The program must be resourceful. Agents and managers should be proactive, think ahead, and be ready to improvise when necessary.

- **Cultural and personal fit:** Since executive protection agents are up close and personal with the principal and his or her staff, it's imperative that we fit in. If no one in the corporate environment uses "Sir" or "Ma'am," then we don't either. It's all about not making the principal miss a beat: we must live and breathe as if we are a part of the organizational culture—because we are.

- **Calm sense of urgency:** Everyone in the service industry knows that good service is always time-sensitive; in our field it can be critical. Nonetheless, it is imperative that executive protection providers never create unnecessary nervousness and that they keep things under control even in the face of surprises.

- **Attention to detail:** Many of the little things we do can have major repercussions—both because of what we do and for whom we do it.

- **Controlled empathy:** We do everything we can to keep our principal safe, happy and productive. But sometimes the principal's security takes precedence. We're prepared to act on this even when it's not the most popular thing to do.

- **Collaboration:** Relationships with others in the corporate organization affect the program's efficiency, and thus both the principal's experience and security. Executive protection agents and managers can rarely pull rank to do what they need to do within the organization, so they have to earn respect and cooperation rather than rely on authority.

Policies and procedures make it operational

Once you've defined the standards against which you want to develop your corporate executive protection program, it's time to set your sites on developing relevant policies and procedures.

Policies are written documents that express how the executive protection organization will deal with all key issues that impact program deliverables and adherence to agreed standards. Procedures are the step-by-step instructions that dictate how some aspects of some policies are implemented; standard operating procedures, or SOPs, typically refer to critical procedures from which deviation is least tolerated.

Establishing clear policies for executive protection programs is helpful for many reasons. These are some:

- Policies ensure compliance with any relevant regulations and are explicit interpretations of the program's agreed standards.

- They enable program-wide consistency, even in times of change, so that decisions are made in a uniform way in the field and at home.

- They establish a clear understanding of roles, responsibilities and accountability, and facilitate reliable performance assessment.

We believe all corporate executive protection programs should have policies and procedures that govern the following areas:

- Policies that impact legal affairs

  — Confidentiality

  — Use of force

  — Insurance

  — Contracts

- HR-related policies

  — Physical fitness

  — Training

  — Career development

  — Performance assessment

  — Substance abuse

  — Vetting and background checks

  — Remuneration, pension, benefits

  — Internet, email, social media

- Financial policies

  — Budget planning

  — Expense reporting

- Travel policies

- Detail policies

  — Advance work

  — Coverage of the principal

    - At home

    - At work

    - While commuting

    - While traveling

- Reporting policies

  — Key metrics and KPIs

  — Trip/detail reporting

  — Monthly/quarterly/yearly reporting

- Vendor and procurement policies

  — Make/buy decisions

  — Vendor approval

  — Vetting and control

Best practice: Use it or lose it

Corporate executive protection policies and procedures are only useful if they are prepared well and used consistently. Here are a few things we have learned along the way.

- **Ownership and approval:** Be clear on who owns the policy and who needs to be involved in its approval. While executive protection policies are usually developed by the executive protection manager, the chief security officer (CSO) will certainly want to be involved in making sure they are in line with overall security policies. Similarly, it is natural to reach out to corporate HR, Legal, Finance, Procurement and other departments to ensure the EP policies comply with corporate standards.

- **Communication and training:** Everyone impacted by a policy should have easy access to it and the opportunity to learn everything relevant about it. Sounds obvious, but it isn't always. Also, it is often not enough that staff are simply exposed to written versions of a policy. Careful training procedures let employees test and improve their understanding of policies and procedures.

- **Review:** All policies should be reviewed on a regular basis to determine compliance and relevance. If the level of compliance is not acceptable, then there is something wrong with either team performance or the policy itself; in either case, management must do something. If the policy is never used or is deemed to no longer have relevance, then it should be deleted.

Chapter 7:
The benefits of outsourcing executive services compared to trying to build internal competencies

Make or buy? The decision belongs to the corporation, of course. And we're fully aware that we can be accused of tooting our own horn in this chapter. But we think there are some compelling reasons why practically all corporations choose to outsource executive protection services, at least in part, to specialist partners rather than exclusively trying to build internal competencies in this niche profession.

Of course we're always open to new business, but whether the corporation ends up working with us or with one of our competitors doesn't matter in terms of this chapter. What does matter is the safety, productivity and satisfaction of the principal, and the viability of the executive protection program. We've yet to meet the corporation that has set up a successful executive protection program using exclusively its own full-time employees. In fact, we've been called in to turn around several such programs that the corporation started and then gave up on.

Specialist executive protection expertise is impossible for the corporation to match

Specialist partners are, well, specialists.

Their management teams have hands-on experience in corporate executive protection that can be decades long. They have operating procedures that have proven their worth in practice. They know how to recruit and develop agents who go on to have success. And the skills they've learned in working for one corporation, they can transfer to another.

Unlike an organization that is building its own executive protection program from scratch, specialist partners that serve many clients are able to benchmark against other programs. They have a hard-earned sense of what constitutes best industry practice. And they bring this to their clients in many ways, from program design and implementation to full or partial staffing.

Specialist partners enable speedy implementation and adaptation

A specialist partner is able to implement in less than 48 hours what would take an inexperienced corporation months: put in place a fully functional executive protection program that keeps the principal safe, happy and productive wherever the job or personal interests take him or her. Given the backdrop of why we do what we do—often tangible threats to the principal's well-being—fast program implementation can be a necessity, not a luxury.

Specialist partners are also able to respond rapidly to evolving program needs. Should the program need to be scaled up, domestically or internationally, to cover other principals or to provide more protection in more places, this can be done without lengthy onboarding and training processes. Other services such as event security, secure travel logistics and intelligence analysis can be added immediately.

Similarly, if the program should need to be scaled back for whatever reason, then this can be done straightaway and without concern for severance compensation.

Specialist partners lighten the burden on corporate HR

Another beneficiary of outsourcing part or all of the executive protection program is the corporate HR function. Executive protection is not a core competence of any Fortune 500 corporation. While the safety and productivity of the corporation's leading principals are important, of course, the talent required to provide these will rarely rank very high on the HR department's list of priorities.

To staff and run an executive protection program on its own, the corporation would need to become expert in sourcing, interviewing, security screening, training and developing, compensating, and onboarding and offboarding of executive protection managers and agents—just to mention a few HR issues. Most corporations prefer not to use headcount or dedicate HR expertise to such non-core, specialized services.

The situation is of course different for specialist executive providers. They have a vested interest and experience in finding candidates that have the best chance for long-term success. They appreciate the need for developing people and skills, and are accustomed to ensuring that all agents have an annual training program including drills, tabletops and recurring basic training to keep perishable skills fresh. They can provide advanced development training designed to increase agent capabilities and performance quality. And they know the importance of spotting talent and encouraging the best to follow career paths of growing expertise and responsibility.

Specialist partners have a deep bench of pre-screened and vetted candidates for executive protection agent and manager positions. If one does not work out—for whatever reason—the person can be changed quickly and efficiently. What is more, specialist partners have immediate access to a worldwide professional network of closely-vetted vendors, enabling them to provide complementary services globally.

Using special partners can also reduce the corporation's legal exposure and eliminate the need for special licensing and insurance coverage. Professional executive protection companies will have their own use-of-force policies, potentially obviating the corporation's need for such.

Professionalism that trumps corporate politics

Executive protection is by its very nature up close and personal. If the principal becomes dissatisfied with a manager or agent for whatever reason, this might compromise the program and the principal's security and productivity. It is therefore imperative that the principal not hesitate, due to respect for the executive protection agent's feelings or corporate HR practices, to initiate termination of a person with whom he or she is not comfortable.

Since the principal often spends more time with executive protection agents than with his or her senior management team (and definitely more time than with the corporation's security director or chief security officer), the position of executive protection agent carries perceived power and heightened responsibility. Agents must be of a special psychological makeup to handle their role.

It can be unfair to put an employee in that situation. Specialist partners have better conditions for handling this sensitive situation than corporate employees, because they must treat *everyone* in the client organization as a customer—not just the CEO. This encourages cooperation and harmony rather than favoritism and rivalry.

Specialist partners have transparent costs

Are the executive protection services to be paid for by the client company, or will the principal pay for some of the costs? Often, the answer is both. This can present the corporation with accounting challenges—and lead to gaps in security for the principal. The utilization of a specialist partner provides seamless protection services regardless of whether the corporation or its employee is footing the bill. Costs can be more easily segregated between business and personal use when services are provided by a specialist partner.

Cost is another reason that corporations sometimes consider setting up their own executive protection programs. But when they analyze the "total costs of ownership" of establishing and running an executive protection program, i.e., including all costs associated with recruitment, training, bonuses, stock options, benefits, turnover, etc., then many discover that in addition to all of the other advantages, outsourcing executive protection is also cost-competitive.

From one-off projects to embedded agents to full-time employee: Flexibility is key

When it comes to executive protection, corporations tackle the make-buy issue in many ways. But we do see some similarities.

One-off and special projects, such as taking care of a principal on trips to selected destinations, will always be fully outsourced.

Comprehensive programs that provide more complete executive protection are often 100 percent outsourced initially, as the corporate security department has neither the expertise nor other resources to establish the program on its own. This will typically include consulting on program setup, outsourced executive protection agents and/or residential security agents, and an outsourced executive protection manager.

As the program matures, the corporation may choose to make the executive protection manager its own full-time employee, with or without consulting support from a specialist partner. Doing so squarely places the executive protection function on the corporation's organizational chart, establishes the function as a corporate priority, and enables the corporate executive protection manager to be a fully integrated part of the corporation's security setup. Some executive protection and residential security agents may also become full-time employees, while others will be fully embedded.

Embedding executive protection agents and managers and intelligence analysts has its own advantages. These persons will live and breathe in the corporate ecosystem, but will also have the benefits of being able to draw on the specialist partner's network of expertise. Fully mature corporate executive protection programs are often a hybrid of full-time employees and employees embedded from a specialist partner.

Chapter 8:
How to write an RFP for corporate executive protection services

Every good corporate executive protection program starts with a good RFP. Or should, at least.

Because the RFP, or request for proposal, is the most powerful document the corporation has to structure the bidding process and improve the transparency of competing bidders' advantages and disadvantages.

All organizations have their own purchasing policies and procedures, and most will probably already have guidelines and templates regarding RFPs. But few corporations have much experience in outsourcing such a specialist partner service as executive protection. Given the executive protection program's up-close-and-personal visibility with top execs, this experience gap matters: Whereas most purchasing decisions made by the security department will not figure prominently on the CEO's radar, the people chosen to provide close personal protection will.

In this chapter, we provide an outline of the various elements a good RFP should contain. It will allow you to organize your RFP so that it makes clear the decision criteria you apply in choosing your executive protection partner. And it will enable you to ask the right questions to make an informed decision.

Price is inevitably one of the most scrutinized of all the many criteria, and of course it matters. But we would encourage organizations to broaden the scope of the RFP well beyond price. We've been called in to fix a number of programs that started out with low-cost vendors but ended up costing far more than they should have. In executive protection like anything else, you get what you pay for. But unlike many other purchases, the costs of a failed executive protection program can be much greater than purely financial.

Scoring and weighting according to well-defined decision criteria

We think it's a good idea to lay out the decision criteria in clusters, weight each of them according to relative importance, then score your evaluation of each vendor bid, for example as in the table on the next page. It's also a good idea to inform vendors of your criteria and how you intend to weight them.

Criteria	Weight	A	B	C
Company background/ management	10			
Protective service capabilities	10			
Human resource management	20			
Protective service processes	20			
Implementation plan	10			
References	10			
Price	20			
Total	100			

Statement of Work/Scope of Work

The statement of work (SOW) should make clear just what kinds of protective services the corporation wants to contract. But realistically, it can be difficult or impossible for corporations with no experience in executive protection to know exactly what they need.

How extensive does the Risk, Threat and Vulnerability Assessment (RTVA) need to be? How often should it be updated? Are advance trips to upcoming travel destinations always necessary? Why or why not? Should intelligence analysis be part of the program?

Answers to these and many more questions can be elusive for non-experts. That's why some corporations rely on external consultants to carry out an RTVA and make SOW recommendations based on the results.

The SOW should cover at least all these basic points:

- Who: Principal(s) to be protected

- What: Specific tasks
  - Threat assessments
  - Advance work
  - Security driving
  - Close protection
    - Office
    - Residential
  - Travel logistics
- When: Full-time, part-time
- Where:
  - Office
  - Residential
  - Travel
  - Domestic
  - International
- How:
  - Specific tasks
  - Procedures
  - Operational planning
  - Staffing and training
  - SOPs
  - Quality control/KPIs
  - Reporting

— Contingency/response plans

— Stakeholder communication

— Expense reporting and invoicing

— Personnel and program evaluation

— Key personnel needed from vendor

Vendor background information

Once you have defined the scope of work, you're ready to start asking potential vendors to bid on it. The next thing to do is to get vendors to provide information that will let you evaluate their expertise and ultimately let you choose among them.

The first cluster of decision criteria lets you examine some of the basics: you need to get some general background information from all vendors.

Financial information: Ask all bidders to provide information that proves their company is a viable business. Are they profitable? Are they growing? Can you count on them to be around in a year? To find out, you should go back at least three years and require bidders to provide balance sheets and income statements, at least.

Management team: Good companies have good management. Ask for the management team's bios or CVs. Find out which person at the senior executive level will be accountable for your program. If the scope of work calls for a team or on-site manager, you'll also want to learn more about who the vendor proposes for this important role.

Mission, values and guiding principles: Try to move beyond all the marketing talk and get a good sense of what makes the vendor tick. What kind of values do they try to instill throughout their company? Do they have a set of guiding principles that are clear and actionable? Do they walk the talk?

Compliance with ethical, environmental and other corporate purchasing guidelines: We've seen it happen time and again: The security director puts together an RFP as best he can and sends it to potential vendors; then the purchasing department asks for a whole slew of other information in keeping with corporate purchasing guidelines.

Be sure to ask about whatever is relevant for your corporation. Some of the more common guidelines include:

- **Quality control:** What kinds of quality assurance programs does the vendor use? Are they certified according to ISO 9000 or 9001 standards?

- **Environmental:** Does the vendor comply with corporate environmental standards? What kinds of certifications does it use to ensure compliance?

- **Nondiscrimination:** How does the vendor ensure compliance with nondiscrimination policies regarding gender, race, etc.? For larger programs, how can they ensure that the diversity of the corporate workforce is also reflected in the protective team?

- **Anti-corruption/bribery:** What are the vendor's policies regarding corruption, bribery, etc.? For example, do managers and agents receive training in the UK Bribery Act or other accepted ways of preventing bribery?

Global presence: Seamless quality of service regardless of location is a hallmark of good executive protection, and you will want to understand the vendor's ability to provide protection and smooth logistics worldwide.

This is worth considering even if the scope of work currently calls for protection in only one country (exceedingly rare in a globalized economy). Protection needs change, sometimes quickly; you want your executive protection vendor to scale internationally as and when necessary. Ask to learn more about the vendor's

- **Own locations:** Where do they have people, offices or subsidiaries?

- **Vetted vendor/partner locations:** Where do they have tested, tried and true partners?

- **Vendor vetting procedures:** What are their procedures for selecting, training and briefing other companies in other territories? How do they carry out remote supervision? How do you know the "security driver" they provide in Karachi is reliable, and that you can safely entrust your CEO to his driving skills and background?

Insurance: How is the vendor's liability and other insurance coverage? Be sure to get some insight into the kind and level of insurance protection.

Licensing: Licensing requirements vary internationally and by state in the U.S. Ask vendors to provide information on what kinds of licenses allow it to operate where.

Vendor protective service capabilities

When choosing an executive protection provider, it's important to gain a comprehensive overview of the bidding vendors' capabilities. That they all can build and deliver a basic executive protection program should be a given. Therefore, you will as a minimum want to examine their expertise concerning protective agents, security drivers and program management.

In order to future-proof your vendor relationship, however, it is a good idea to look beyond the minimum requirements. You need to ask questions about related security services, too.

- Can they provide you with **strategic planning support** in addition to tactical implementation?

- Do they have experience in **residential security**? How do they recommend aligning residential security services with the rest of the executive protection program?

- If the need arises, can they ramp up security with **protective surveillance** or **countersurveillance** teams?

- What is their track record in adding **intelligence analysis** to protective programs? How would they recommend staffing, managing and integrating the intel piece into the overall program?

- Can they also provide **event security**? Depending on the corporation's needs, it might make good business sense to ask the same vendor to handle executive protection and event security services.

- What about **corporate investigations**?

When considering all of these protective service capabilities, it important to consider vendors as long-term partners with whom you will be building and maintaining the program. Unlike other security services, executive protection is intimately entwined with the principal's daily routines and the corporate culture. Once implemented, there is a resistance to making major changes, so choosing the best partner from the beginning is even more important here than in other areas with less direct involvement with the principal.

Human resource management

Executive protection is a people business.

While this is true for many industries, the up-close-and-personal nature of executive protection makes human resource management an especially critical decision criterion. The RFP process should enable the corporation to understand how vendors manage HR because a provider's ability to recruit, develop and retain the best people is essential to program success.

Scope: The first thing to look at is the kinds of employees the vendor can provide. Depending on the nature of the program, you may need to fill some or all of the jobs listed below, and you want to be sure that your vendor has the necessary experience and expertise in providing quality people. How do they recruit, vet, develop and retain these specialists?

- EP agents

- Protective surveillance agents

- Security drivers

- EP managers

- Residential security agents

- Intelligence analysts

- Event security specialists

- Corporate investigators

Vetting process: You should ask tough questions about how the vendor vets potential candidates for each job type. What policies and procedures do they follow in order to ensure that those charged with protecting the principal are worthy of this trust?

"Background checks" can be bought off the shelf, and some vendors are satisfied with low-cost but superficial versions of these. Others have far more thorough processes that might include anything from extensive and recurring reference checks to social media analyses and even polygraph tests.

Hard skills and experience: A variety of trainable, demonstrable skills is essential to good executive protection. These vary according to the specific job type.

You will want to understand how the vendor sets standards for training and experience for each and every job type called for in the scope of work:

- What are the minimum **training qualifications** for each job type? Which courses must candidates have completed? From which type of training school?

- How many **years of relevant experience** are necessary for each job type?

- Ask to see job descriptions and required qualifications for each job type.

- What are the providers' policies for **refreshing perishable skills**? For many skill sets, including critical ones like evasive driving and emergency medical care, it's *use it or lose it*: providers who aren't requiring their staff to do regular training aren't doing their job.

- **Certifications:** Does the vendor have company-wide quality assurance certifications such as ISO 9001? What certifications are necessary to fulfill specific job types?

Soft skills: As we point out in Chapter 9, the mastery of hard skills is a necessary but insufficient qualification for success in an executive protection job. Emotional intelligence is equally important. Why? Because if the people providing the protection 24/7 don't thoroughly understand and adapt to both the corporate culture and the principal's personal preferences, it is unlikely that the program will achieve sustainable success.

To thrive in executive protection, it is necessary for drivers, agents and managers to possess a variety of characteristics we call "soft skills." To mention a few: resilience, empathy, discretion and self-awareness. While all of these can be improved by dedicated effort, they are essentially personality traits that some people possess more than others.

The context of the RFP is too narrow to investigate the psychological makeup of potential agents. Still, it is a good opportunity to discover how seriously vendors take this critical aspect of the business, so at least a few good questions are in order:

- What are the provider's procedures for ensuring a good cultural fit between protective agents and corporate stakeholders? What do they actually do to learn about the corporate culture and adapt programs accordingly?

- How does the provider make sure that the program meet's the principal's personal preferences? What are the procedures for discovering these, and for making sure they are respected across three-shift teams and around the world?

- What procedures does the provider use to evaluate the soft skills of its candidates? How does it match individual agents and managers to individual clients?

Employee continuity: The security industry is notorious for high staff turnover and low employee loyalty. This has negative consequences for the quality of its services and for the reputation of the entire industry.

While the executive protection sector is better off in this regard than many other parts of the industry, we too can get better. For far too many years, we in executive protection have failed to give our employees the means to develop their careers. We have not been good enough at nurturing talent through career planning, and we have paid the price: too many high performers have switched companies to climb up a rung of the career ladder, and too many low performers have stayed where they are.

While it's not the corporation's headache to organize a supplier's HR efforts, if it is interested in sustainable program success it will want to enquire how the vendor does so.

Be sure to ask how the vendor ensures staff continuity through employee retention and career planning. Two simple metrics that are useful: employee turnover rate and average years of employment.

Employee compensation and benefits: It is a fair question in the RFP process to ask how the vendor pays its employees.

Transparency around employee compensation and benefits (including 401(k), health, life, vision, dental, short-term disability, long-term disability, paid time off, performance bonuses, etc.) is important. Because everything else being equal, vendors who provide competitive salary and benefit packages are more likely to attract the best talent. We have yet to work for a client who doesn't want the best talent when it comes to close protection.

Scalability/surge capacity: Extending the program's scope means adding resources, and corporations need to consider vendors' ability to scale up quickly if this becomes necessary. Adding another principal to the program could effectively double the staff needed. Can the vendor respond quickly? How? What kinds of lead times are necessary?

Vendor protective service processes

You will want to pay particular attention to how vendors organize the nuts and bolts of their services. All the bullet points below are important, and you should ask vendors to provide information on the procedures and processes they use for all of them.

Who does what? When and with what frequency? How do they actually do it? What information do they supply? What is expected of you in each process? Where will you need to approve or review?

- Risk, Threat and Vulnerability Analyses (RTVA)

- Operational planning

- Staffing and training

- Standard Operating Procedures (SOPs)

- Quality control/KPIs

- Reporting

- Contingency/response plans

- Stakeholder communication

- Expense reporting and invoicing

- Personnel and program evaluation

All of the above points are important but we want to call out one in particular for our friends in corporate security: reporting.

Like any other expense the corporation commits to, executive protection is an investment that will be scrutinized in many ways. Security directors can be hard-pressed to demonstrate the return on investment of an executive protection program: If nothing happened to the principal either before or after program implementation, then what difference has the program made?

Good reporting based on solid data can help security directors quantify program value. You should ask vendors to tell what kind of data they can and will report, how they will do it, and with what frequency.

Implementation plan

A great way to learn how a company works is to ask them to describe how they would implement the new program. What are the process milestones? When can you expect these to be achieved? Who on the vendor side will be involved—and who on the corporate side will need to be involved?

References

Last but by no means least are client references. Have the

vendors provided similar services for similar clients? How did things go? Are they still providing services? Why or why not?

Of course, no serious executive protection company would list corporate or other clients on a website, so you will need to ask. Go beyond the logo lineup and simple client list. Ask to contact one or more of the security directors or CSOs they work for directly, so you can learn firsthand of their experiences with, and opinion of, the vendor.

Price schedule

Ask vendors to break down all costs so that you can see how they arrive at a total. Compare competing bids at the line-item level. Be sure to capture all costs—both fixed and variable, ongoing, out of pocket, etc.—and to understand what is and is not included in the budget.

RFP schedule/timing

Depending on the complexity of the scope of work, the RFP process can take anywhere from a week to several months. Be sure to allocate enough time for vendors and your own purchasing department (PD) to prepare and complete all these steps:

1. PD issues request for proposal and sets due dates for clarification requests, clarification responses, notification of intent to bid, and proposal submission.

2. Vendors request RFP clarification by due date.

3. PD responds to clarification requests by due date.

4. Vendors submit notice of intent to bid by due date.

5. Vendors submit proposals by due date.

6. PD schedules, and vendors make, oral presentations.

7. PD awards contract in time for expected start date of work.

Part II:
Corporate EP
management

Introduction to Part II: Managing corporate executive protection

While practically all Fortune 500 and many other companies will have either a Chief Security Officer (CSO) or someone at the VP or senior director level filling a similar role, the role of "Executive Protection Manager" is still unheard of in many organizations. Either they don't have any kind of executive protection program, or their perceived executive protection requirements are too small or fragmented to justify this specialist position. These companies might hire external support on an ad hoc basis, for example for travel to risky territories or event security, but they do not provide anyone in the company with full-time executive protection services.

This is changing fast, however. As corporations begin to understand the necessity and benefits of executive protection, and provide it for one or more persons (typically beginning at the

CEO, COO or CFO level), the need for dedicated executive protection management arises. And with this need, the realization that no one in the organization, including the CSO, knows enough about executive protection to actually develop and manage a program.

This is not a project that the CSO can simply delegate to HR. In our experience, corporate HR departments have a difficult time with executive protection programs. Human resource specialists typically have no experience in what is admittedly a very narrow niche. They do not know how to organize and staff an executive protection department. They struggle to identify the talent necessary to manage and operate executive protection programs. Setting salaries is a mystery. Unfortunately, the importance of ongoing training, even though nothing ever happens to the principal, often eludes them.

The special role of the corporate executive protection manager

The role of the corporate executive protection manager is like that of any other manager. Except it's different.

Corporate executive protection managers can be tasked with running programs that have neither successful precedents nor useful performance benchmarks. The role is highly visible to the CEO, his or her closest associates and top-tier executives, and even family—but it is not a high-level position. And like any other manager, corporate executive protection managers must navigate the demands of those further up the hierarchy and adhere to corporate values, strategies and budget guidelines— while at the same make hard decisions about subordinates and maintain a motivated, high-performing team.

The manager is inevitably seen as the face, hands and brains of the executive protection program. Right or wrong, all eyes look to the manager when there is something broken that needs to get fixed. But in addition to being responsible for the nuts and bolts of daily operations, the manager must also function as the program's ambassador and evangelist, building relationships where none have existed before and educating the organization about what EP is and isn't.

Both hard and soft skills are necessary

To accomplish all of this requires a generalist with specialist competencies and a unique set of personal attributes. Just like the head coach of a professional sports team, the executive protection manager must possess consummate understanding of all aspects of the game, including its hard and soft skills. The executive protection manager must be a player's player who knows what it takes to make all the parts fit together, just as eager and able to take on a blocking role or make an assist as to run back the kickoff or take a shot on goal. And he or she must imbue the entire team with this same attitude and approach: it's not about making the individual players happy, it's about the team winning in its efforts to keep the principal safe, happy and productive.

Since most corporations are not familiar with executive protection from a human resources point of view, we begin this section of our book with a look at the particular skillsets that executive protection managers—and the agents they manage—need to possess.

Chapter 9 describes the hard skills, the kinds of things that can be learned through training and experience, that are peculiar to our industry.

In Chapter 10, we examine the personality traits to look for in successful executive protection agents, and, by extension, in their managers. While these attributes can of course be further developed through concerted efforts, it is important to note that an individual who is conspicuously lacking in these social and emotional competences is unlikely to thrive in corporate executive protection.

Consistency is key

Good executive protection managers know that consistent performance, in the long run, is worth more than stretches of so-so deliveries punctuated by occasional displays of brilliance. The ability to repeat successes, as a team, is critical.

If the principal likes to run and needs protection on his daily jogs, then it's not enough to have just one executive protection agent on the team who is a capable runner and can keep up. This would eventually lead to favoritism and imbalance, and jeopardize overall team performance. It is up to the executive protection manager to discover the principal's personal preferences, then compose a team that can respect these—and best practices for executive protection—day in, day out— regardless of whether it's a question of collecting the dry-cleaning or planning a multi-continent itinerary for multiple principals.

Taking a lesson from Peter Drucker

While no books have been written about corporate *executive protection* management, thousands have been published on management as such. And few have had the influence on generations of managers as the work of Peter Drucker.

We have no pretension of being in the same league as Drucker. But we will allow ourselves to borrow from his straightforward and time-tested explanation of the manager's job, and adapt his description of the manager's five key tasks to corporate executive protection: setting objectives, organizing, motivating and communicating, measurement and people development.

In Chapter 11 we look at what types of goals the executive protection manager needs to set for the team.

Chapter 12 discusses the options facing corporations on how to organize their executive protection program. Here, we will outline the organizational trajectory through which most corporate executive protection programs progress as they mature.

One of the most common employee complaints in any organization is poor communication from their managers. Corporate executive protection is no different. In Chapter 13, we examine the importance of clear communication between managers and agents, and between those directly involved in the program and others in the corporate ecosystem.

Chapter 14 digs into how to measure the corporate executive protection team's performance, and proposes a number of KPIs that program managers should consider.

Finally, we round off Drucker's five key tasks and this section of the book in Chapter 15, where we lay out some important considerations for managers about how to develop people, so that the careers of those who are ablest develop accordingly, and the corporate executive protection program continues to improve in quality and productivity.

Chapter 9:
The hard skills and experience necessary for corporate executive protection

As the corporate executive protection industry becomes more professional, so do the requirements for agents and managers.

The level of experience and skills required to work as a corporate executive protection agent exceeds those of the rest of the security industry. Candidates need real-life security experience just to get in the door, and dedicated training and certifications to move up. And as we will see in the next chapter, they need to have a special mix of soft skills to become high performers and move into management.

But first, let us concentrate on the training and experience that constitute the "hard" skills.

Executive protection training is necessary for everyone in the industry

No matter what the candidate's background, specialized executive protection training is a prerequisite for work in corporate executive protection. The skills learned here are different than those developed in law enforcement, the military or other security-related fields. The good schools are run by professionals who have real-life executive protection experience and are also great teachers.

Below is what we look for in an executive protection agent's training history:

- **Basic executive protection school:** These introductory courses are offered by a number of private schools and vary in length and quality.

- **Emergency medical training:** Executive protection professionals must be trained in cardiopulmonary resuscitation (CPR) and automated external defibrillator (AED) use and have first aid training at the healthcare-provider level to operate in our industry.

- **Evasive/antiterrorism driving:** The ability to safely operate a motor vehicle is of paramount importance in executive protection, and "security drivers" and "executive protection drivers" are some of the most valuable functions on any team. It's often the first position on a team.

- **Defensive tactics:** The particular method, or mix of methods, is not as important as "cover and evacuate" rather than a "stay and fight" mind-set.

- **Foreign language skills:** The ability to get by in other cultures is vital to international executive protection, and speaking more than one language is always an advantage.

- **Protective advance work:** Unfortunately, most executive protection schools do not spend enough time on protective advance work, so we ask candidates how they have otherwise acquired and developed these skills.

- **Firearms:** Armed corporate executive protection details are extremely rare in the United States and the rest of the world. In the relatively few cases where executive protection details are armed, however, it's important to note that the use of firearms is very different from other armed security, law enforcement or military roles. Those relatively few persons who do participate in armed executive protection details require a radically different kind of training than that required in other armed roles.

Additional recommended courses:

- Transitional training for law enforcement, military and high-threat protection specialists

- Covert executive protection

- Surveillance detection

- Etiquette training

- Event management training

Many kinds of experience can lead to a career in executive protection

People with many different kinds of backgrounds make excellent careers in corporate EP. Indeed, in our experience, success in corporate executive protection depends primarily on the individual, not on his or her former career. We've seen rookies become professionals quickly, and we've seen seasoned professionals do a horrible job. Below are some of the most common backgrounds for corporate executive protection:

- **Security:** Typically, people with experience in security positions such as uniformed, plainclothes, residential, commercial, government or nonprofit. People with these backgrounds usually start executive protection at the entry level but can easily go on to become great success stories and enjoy excellent careers in executive protection.

- **Law enforcement:** The law enforcement officers (LEOs) we see come from federal, state or local agencies. The executive protection industry gets some immediate gratification from people with this background:

  — Ability to drive extremely well

  — Local knowledge

  — Ability to deal with difficult people and de-escalate conflicts through verbal means

  — Defensive tactics

  — Natural ability to protect.

  LEOs who have not served in a dignitary or elected official protective detail must usually start out in entry-level positions. Because of the skills mentioned above, however, they usually do not stay at the entry level for very long.

- **Military:** Since the military community is a massive entity, we see applicants from every branch and virtually every function. The veterans who seem to do really well don't necessarily come from one specific branch or group. The most successful veterans are those who took the skills they learned in the military, then sought out the best private sector training they could find. At the end of the day it always came down to the person and his or her ability to adapt. To adapt to corporate executive protection, good transitional training and an openness to accepting an entry-level position are extremely helpful.

- **High-threat protection:** This includes anyone working in a high-threat protective (HTP) capacity on behalf of a private security agency. Most of these folks have impressive military or law enforcement backgrounds prior to their work in the HTP community. Typically the ones who have the most staying power in corporate executive protection are those who had good transitional training.

- **Dignitary/diplomatic protection:** While this term can cover several groups, we refer specifically to those who have worked in an official capacity for heads of state, royalty, Department of State, etc. As a rule of thumb, this group is suitable for mid-level executive protection positions but would also benefit from a high-quality executive protection course.

- **Celebrity/entertainment protection (aka Hollywood bodyguards):** We have interviewed many individuals from this arena. A few were awesome, and we knew instantly that they would make a smooth transition to corporate executive protection. And then there were the rest. The good ones recognize that corporate executive protection and celebrity protection are different animals. For example, it's very common in Hollywood circles to take pictures with clients, and it's even considered OK to geo-tag current client locations; these would be considered reasons for dismissal in corporate executive protection.

- **Corporate/high-net-worth executive protection:** Of course, these are the jobs we most frequently hire for, and there are applicants who already have good experience in the field. They have experience protecting C-level executives for Fortune 500 and other corporations, and/or experience protecting high-net-worth clients.

Typical qualifications for executive protection positions

Entry level: Minimum qualifications for residential agents and junior EP agents

This is where almost everyone starts a career in dedicated corporate executive protection firms. A background in the military or law enforcement might be enough to get through the gates at smaller local firms, but most larger firms with international clients like to thoroughly vet individuals as they work their way up from residential security or junior protection jobs. This is the best way to evaluate whether they have the mind-set that's needed to handle a mid-level executive protection position.

Certifications/licenses

- Executive protection training course that gives a basic understanding of protective advance work, route planning and fleet management

- Course on defensive tactics in executive protection

- CPR/first aid/AED certified

- Licensed for their specified area of operations

- Valid driver's license

- Valid U.S. or foreign passport

- Be physically fit and have passed a standard Physical Fitness Test (PFT)

- Minimum high school or GED

Experience—must possess at least one of the following

- 1+ year of corporate/high-new-worth executive protection project experience

- 3+ years of residential security experience

- 2+ years of law enforcement experience

- 2+ years of military service

Mid-level: Minimum requirements for EP agents

Candidates who want to be considered for a position as a mid-level agent have the experience that enables them to work on most EP details, and might be on the road to management. Below are typical mid-level standards.

Certifications/Licenses

- Graduate from a reputable executive protection school

- Course on defensive tactics in executive protection

- Emergency medical training (first responder preferred)

- Evasive/antiterrorism driving training

- Licensed for specified area of operations

- Valid driver's license

- Valid U.S. or foreign passport

- Be physically fit and have passed our Physical Fitness Test (PFT)

- Minimum high school or GED

Experience

- 3+ years of corporate, high-net-worth family or other executive protection experience

- Experience working with executive assistants, other corporate functions and key client personnel

- Tangible experience performing dynamic, protective advance operations

- Experience securely transporting clients in all types of ground vehicle operations

- Familiar with private air operations and traveling on short notice

- Proven proficiency in protective intelligence

Other expertise and skills

- Proven interpersonal skills and customer service mind-set

- Proven proficiency in verbal de-escalation of conflicts

- Excellent understanding of local use-of-force laws

- Proven writing and administrative skills, including proficiency in Microsoft Word, Excel and PowerPoint

Senior level: Minimum requirements

Senior-level candidates are suitable for EP manager positions.

At this level, requirements are not as clear cut. As a general rule of thumb, however, applicants at this level will have 7+ years of corporate and/or high-net-worth executive protection experience, as well as at least two years of supervisory experience in those environments.

Along with experience, what generally propels individuals from mid- to senior-level positions is timing, opportunity and their ability to lead.

Corporate executive protection is the ultimate niche market. Real leaders are a niche within the niche. Our industry needs more leaders.

The best corporate executive protection companies work to create leaders as well as successful programs. They encourage employees to grow, move as far as their abilities and drive can take them and have a clear career path in mind.

Chapter 10:
The personality traits to look for in successful corporate executive protection agents

In addition to the hard skills and experience we outlined in Chapter 9, successful executive protection agents possess a number of other characteristics that can be broadly described as soft skills or personality traits.

In this chapter, we outline the 10 traits that set apart high-performing executive protection agents from the less-great. Many are interrelated; all are important. When an individual agent displays most or all of these traits strongly, he or she would make a highly successful executive protection agent—and would also do well in many other fields.

The first five traits are particularly significant for the special demands of the protective service industry. Because our overarching goals are to keep our principals safe, happy and productive no matter where their jobs and other interests take them, we must consistently come up with solutions to new challenges, and we spend a lot of time with principals without being their friends. It requires a certain kind of person to thrive in this context.

The second five traits focus on emotional intelligence (also called EQ), which is also essential for success in corporate EP. Daniel Goleman, who has written extensively on the matter, sums up some key concepts relative to EQ and leadership. We believe these traits apply just as well to EP agents as they do to CEOs.

1. Resourcefulness

A good executive protection agent needs a special mix of smarts and moxie. We call it resourcefulness.

Executive protection teams are often in situations that are completely new. Changes of venue, tasks, expectations and many other aspects of the job are commonplace. Even the best standard operating procedures are tested by nonstandard situations. If there is confusion, the EP agent is the one everyone looks to to make it all good again.

Resourceful executive protection agents make do with what they've got and always try to get the best outcome out of any situation. They're creative problem solvers, adaptive and quick to think on their feet. They ask for what they need—and aren't too shy to ask loudly if that's what's required to get the job done. They always have a Plan B and C. And they never act as if there is anything but Plan A.

The mental habit of thinking ahead is another characteristic of a resourceful executive protection agent, for as Seneca pointed out several thousand years ago, "Luck is what happens when preparation meets opportunity." Good executive protection agents make their own luck—and deliver superior results—through forward thinking. Their approach resembles that of a chess player more than a checkers fan: They are used to thinking several moves ahead so that they can shape outcomes proactively rather than deal reactively with adverse situations. We believe forward thinking is so important to quality executive protection that we have made it one of our guiding principles—and even part of our logo.

2. Resilience

Life is full of stress, and bad things happen—also to good executive protection agents. Resilient executive protection agents aren't the ones who never get into tough situations. We all do that. They're the ones who cope with adversity and keep the mission on track no matter what. Helplessness is never an option.

Psychologically, resilient executive protection agents are able to navigate through emotional turmoil without turning into a shipwreck. They exude a calm sense of urgency whether everything is business as usual or the situation has leapt into emergency mode. They have the skills and the mind-set to counterbalance negative emotions with positive ones. Even when others are succumbing to negativity and pessimism, resilient agents know how and where to dig deep to find more optimism.

3. Professional commitment

Commitment to the task of serving the principal is an essential part of executive protection.

Good executive protection agents realize that the security, privacy and productivity of the principal come first, and that the needs of the principal supersede their own needs. They are able to put their personal preferences aside and stand by the client no matter what—before, during and after the detail. The same extends toward the rest of the executive protection team.

Successful executive protection agents also realize that this form of professional commitment has nothing to do with the interpersonal commitment that couples promise each other. Professional commitment is a one-way street. It's not reciprocal, and it's not about being the friend of the principal. It's about doing the job we are tasked to do in the most professional way possible.

4. Discretion

Executive protection agents doing close protection of a principal are, well, close to the principal. That closeness extends to all kinds of situations that never can be taught at an executive protection school. In addition to protecting principals as they conduct business, agents will often be there when the principal is traveling, enjoying time with family and friends, and just getting on with his or her life. Complete confidentiality is expected in all matters.

Through it all, good executive protection professionals must maintain their integrity and know their place. Sometimes it's in the foreground and the principal wants to talk; often it's in the background, and the principal has no need to be reminded of his or her board-mandated 24/7 protection services

5. Service-mindedness

Executive protection is a service industry. It's about helping other people (notably, the paying client who has other options) to meet their needs. It's not about you meeting your needs.

If executive protection agents are not comfortable working in a job where the needs of the client take precedence over their own, then they should start looking for other work. Because 95 percent of what we do in corporate executive protection is directly related to taking care of the client's requirements for protection, productivity, comfort and overall well-being. The other 15 percent of the time is spent writing up after-action reviews and expense reports. (Yes, we've noticed that it adds up to more than 100 percent. See the notes on work/life balance below.)

While executive protection agents might sometimes stay at five-star hotels and eat at three-star Michelin restaurants, they are also the ones who clean up before the principal arrives and make sure there's plenty of the principal's favorite water in the car. They may have even washed the car between bites of a plastic sandwich.

Some people get the service mentality, others don't. It's not so much about being servile as it is taking ownership of the job and consistently adapting to the client's needs.

Successful executive protection agents do their jobs, and they help others in the corporate ecosystem to do theirs, too. Because they are service minded, they know that if they make the principal's executive assistant, chief of staff, speech manager or others look good, they too will look good—and the principal will be more likely to be safe, happy and productive.

6. Self-awareness

Executive protection professionals must know their strengths as well as their weaknesses. In addition to being clear on their own goals and motivation, they must be able to recognize how their own moods and emotions impact others.

People with a well-developed sense of self-awareness exude self-confidence. They're also able to laugh at themselves, and feel no need to over- or underestimate their own abilities.

7. Self-regulation

Executive protection agents need a high degree of self-regulation in order to stay open to change and deal with new or ambiguous situations. Good self-regulation helps them choose their words carefully—and gives them the option of thinking before reacting.

Great executive protection agents also master another, very particular form of self-regulation. They are able to remain vigilant for hours on end when absolutely nothing is happening. Moment-by-moment situational awareness is key to protection.

8. Social skills

Executive protection agents must be able to work with people and build relationships in order to make things happen. The best agents are born networkers who lay the groundwork of solid connections everywhere from the C-suite to the hotel kitchen. They find common ground where others find barriers, and they build good rapport wherever they can.

They're also excellent communicators who get their message across and have the persuasiveness to get their way more often than not. They can read a principal and a situation; they know when it's time to fade into the background, when it's time to engage in conversation; and they understand the difference between assertiveness and aggression.

9. Empathy

Empathy starts with being aware of other people's feelings, then considering their feelings when we take action. For the executive protection agent, these "other people" include not only the principal, but everyone else in his or her orbit—also other folks on the executive protection team.

Empathic executive protection agents thrive in international corporate settings. They pick up on verbal and nonverbal cues that express an individual's personality, a corporate culture or an entire nation's way of relating and doing business. They recognize the needs of others. And they act accordingly.

But the empathy of good executive protection agents is controlled, not unrestrained. Controlled empathy enables the successful executive protection agent to temper warm compassion with cool calculation. We don't drop protocols to please the principal. We recognize how people are feeling, and we acknowledge those feelings through our actions without losing sight of the overall program objectives.

Here, too, good executive protection agents understand that empathy is not always a two-way street. It's not about us or our feelings; it's about doing the job in the best way possible.

10. Self-motivation

It is variously called drive, initiative, perseverance and being proactive. Highly motivated executive protection agents don't do the job for the money or the recognition. They achieve for the sake of achievement. A self-motivated executive protection agent is a good executive protection agent. He or she maintains an optimistic outlook even when the chips are down. A high degree of motivation means the performance bar is always on the way up, and continual improvement is a way of life for the professional executive protection team.

A different kind of work/life balance

Corporate executive protection is rarely a 9-5 job. The client's needs come first and they can change suddenly.

Balancing the demands of a corporate executive protection work schedule with those of a significant other or young children can be difficult. There is a lot of time on the road, and although the work often seems glamorous and exciting, it can also get lonely. While working, executive protection agents are away from home, sometimes at someone else's house with someone else's children. They might get to go to lots of parties, but they are the designated driver every time.

In order not to get burned out, executive protection agents need to be extremely good at balancing the demands and perks of the job with all the other parts of their lives. They also need well-managed programs, suitably staffed and led, and career opportunities that allow them to develop and grow.

Chapter 11:
Setting objectives for the corporate executive protection program

The overarching purpose of a corporate executive protection program can be boiled down to a simple idea: mitigating risk to the principal to an acceptable level.

But making such a broad statement of purpose operational is a different matter. Just as "maximizing shareholder value" might be a good description of a corporation's overall objectives, the goal is too broad to guide the many managers who are responsible for actually making this happen. Departmental goals need to be aligned with corporate goals, of course, but they must also be specific enough to create results on a daily basis.

So the first responsibility of the corporate executive protection manager is to define program objectives that are clear and actionable to the executive protection team, the principal and all key players in the corporate ecosystem. Even when these goals pull in different directions, good executive protection managers find creative ways to strike a consistent, high-performing equilibrium between them all.

In this chapter, we propose four overall objectives which apply to practically any corporate executive protection program. Specific program objectives should then build on and expand these high-level goals.

Match program deliveries to an ongoing analysis of the principal's profile and the resulting risks, threats and vulnerabilities

Whether they like it or not, corporate leaders are often public figures who get a lot of media attention. Their prominence can in fact be higher than that of politicians or celebrities with significant name recognition—people with whom they would never compare themselves otherwise.

Executive protection programs must consider the principal's profile, as well as any events or changes that could impact that profile (say an initial public offering (IPO) or a major product launch), when setting objectives. It is important that the Risk, Threat and Vulnerability Analysis (RTVA) is not a one-off, static affair. To be truly useful in an ever-changing world, the RTVA must be a dynamic process that continually assesses as many factors as is feasible.

Conceive and implement the program according to best-practice executive protection standards

Continuous operational excellence is a key objective of any executive protection program, and it is the responsibility of the executive protection manager to ensure that the team performs accordingly.

To do this, the executive protection manager must establish standard operating procedures according to industry best practices for all team activities, as well as all metrics and KPIs to ensure that these are kept. These procedures must cover all aspects of protection, from advance work to after-action reviews.

Of course, all of this must take place within the boundaries of available budget. If budgetary constraints impinge on the manager's ability to deliver best-in-class protection, then the manager will have to lobby for more resources—and at the same time find creative ways to work within the budget.

Align the program with corporate objectives, practices and culture

Because executive protection sometimes fits like a round peg into the square hole of corporate routines, it is especially important that the executive protection manager align the program with the corporation's way of doing things.

In order to deliver against this objective, the executive protection manager must have good answers to many questions. How is the company's mission statement best expressed in terms of corporate protection? What are the rules and policies—written and unwritten—that affect the program? Which values, norms and shared assumptions make it easy to provide executive protection—and which make it difficult? How does one best navigate through the organization's formal structures and unofficial power relationships?

We tell new agents working in a corporate executive protection team that one objective is "don't make the principal think." By this, we mean that executive protection agents need to fit naturally within the corporation's way of doing things, aka its culture. For example, saying "Good morning, sir" in an organization where everyone is on a first-name basis with the CEO creates a cumbersome moment that makes the principal think

"Who is this guy?", instead of simply going about his business. We're there to facilitate business, not get in its way.

Carry out the program according to the personal preferences of the principal

Although the CEO's lifestyle choices are unlikely to have any effect on the corporation's accounting practices or sales management procedures, they make a world of difference to the practice of executive protection. And unless the principal's personal preferences are included in the executive protection program's objectives, the program is doomed to fail—simply because the principal doesn't like it.

Executive protection managers must first understand the personal preferences of the principal, then translate these into objectives that the team can work toward. Making these explicit is no easy task, but it is an essential one.

Chapter 12:
Organizing the corporate EP program

In this chapter, we take a closer look at one of the key challenges of corporate executive protection: how to organize the team that will carry out the day-to-day protection of the principal.

All corporate executive protection programs require a certain set of competencies, and will include roughly the same types of job descriptions. They do so differently, however, according to program complexity and maturity. All corporate executive protection programs will require that the roles below be fulfilled at one level or another. Any serious program should start with at least those roles with an asterisk as must-have elements.

- Executive protection manager*

- Security driver

- Executive protection agents*

- Residential protection agent

- Protective intelligence agent*

- Operations center agents

- Specialist executive protection partner*

Using specialist partners* as part of the protection team

We have included the role of specialist executive protection partner on this must-have role list for a reason: unless you are planning for operations on the scale of the U.S. president's Secret Service, it is simply not feasible to insource all aspects of a modern executive protection program.

This is most readily apparent with something like security drivers. While it might make good sense to hire a full-time security driver based at corporate headquarters, for example, it would be neither efficient nor safe for a corporate program to bring drivers from the United States to India and Nepal for a short business trip. Local road conditions and traffic cultures are radically different, and a U.S. driver couldn't be expected to acquire the linguistic, cultural, navigational and driving skills necessary to do the job properly for a three-day, two-country visit. What does make sense is using a specialist partner who can arrange for vetted security drivers, in many different places, who live up to the same high standards as those applied at home. A reliable specialist partner with global reach can be expected to coordinate such services and others.

Drawing on specialist partners is a reliable way to respond quickly to changing circumstances—which may well be the one constant of a busy executive protection program. If the principal's threat level suddenly increases, specialist partners can be drawn upon to fill the agent gap until more a permanent solution is found or until the threat subsides. Similarly, specialist partners with well-established international networks can allow the program to scale flexibly, globally and quickly, without adding headcount.

The executive protection manager*

The executive protection manager translates strategy into operations; leads and organizes the protection team; and acts as the bridge between the protection team, the principal and the corporate ecosystem. The manager is the one point of contact that all stakeholders look to—and hold responsible for—all aspects of the program.

Depending on the scope of the program, the role of executive protection manager can be filled in a variety of ways. But it should always be filled: it is essential that one person have overall responsibility for the program, and that this is clear to the chief security officer (CSO), the rest of the executive protection team, the principal, and other stakeholders throughout the corporation.

Initially, a brand-new corporate program might bring in a specialist partner on a consultant basis to act as part-time program manager and help set up the program. This has the advantage of using a skilled practitioner who can draw on experience from other corporate programs. Once the program is ready to be implemented, a solution that provides ongoing resources will be necessary.

Some programs might take another approach in their early stages, and go the route of retaining one person with the dual role of local security driver and executive protection coordinator, but not manager. When this person is not driving, he or she is able to work on other aspects of the program, such as liaising with a specialist partner to hire security drivers in other locations.

Once the decision to create a more comprehensive corporate executive protection program has been made, the best way to begin organizing it is to assign it a manager. It will then be the manager's responsibility to ensure that the program is based on an up-to-date Risk, Threat and Vulnerability Analysis, write a suitable strategy, plan and organize program implementation, staff up, and ultimately run the program. Of course, all of this must be done with respect for the corporation's culture and the principal's personal preferences, and in cooperation with the key stakeholders described in Chapter 4.

The manager can be either hired directly by the corporation or "embedded" from a specialist partner. This second option has the advantage of placing the onus of recruiting and developing a new manager on an organization that has a proven track record and deep bench for doing just that—something few corporate security or HR departments have any experience in.

The ideal executive protection manager will be a person with the right background and personality, who has come up through the ranks as a protection agent and understands all practical aspects of the profession, and who has experience in running programs in corporate settings.

A manager will often take a shift as a protection agent for a number of reasons. This could be to fill the occasional scheduling gap, and should be to stay close to the front lines in order to evaluate program and agent performance. The manager needs to discover and correct any issues that can affect program goals, and coach agents accordingly.

At the same time, it is important that the roles of manager and agent not be conflated. If the manager falls into the trap of becoming the default, more-or-less permanent protection agent, then there will be no time to take care of managerial tasks. The manager who continues to act as an agent shirks the work of organizing, planning and maintaining relations across the corporate ecosystem. The tough decisions about hiring, developing and perhaps firing protection agents do not receive the attention they should. Not only does the manager-cum-agent run the clear risk of jeopardizing program success—personal burnout is also all but guaranteed.

Executive protection agents*

A cornerstone of every program, executive protection agents are responsible for providing close protection of the principal. And as discussed in chapters 9 and 10, those who are successful possess a unique mix of hard and soft skills and experience.

These are the persons who create and enforce the actual circle of protection around the principal as he or she moves through the day—both at the office and while traveling. They perform advance work when new locations need to be scouted and made safe. They are on the front line of ongoing security and productivity optimization for the principal, making sure that logistics are as smooth as they can be, and constantly adjusting plans and activities as needs be.

We are often asked how many executive protection agents are necessary to staff a program. Of course, the answer depends on the scope and nature of the program. In our experience, however, at least two full-time agents are needed to create the backbone of a good program, and this can be considered the minimum viable number of dedicated agents. This does not mean that two agents can provide full 24/7/365 coverage for any given principal. It does mean that a minimal team of an executive protection manager and two agents can provide excellent service (with the help of specialist partners as needed) and be a good foundation on which to build.

Such a two-person team is enough to provide solid coverage on a multi-country trip. The manager stays at home, and the two agents leapfrog between destinations. While the first agent is with the principal in one country, the second agent is in the next country doing advance work and double-checking necessary third-party resources such as security drivers, vehicles or additional protective agents sourced through a specialist partner. This second agent stays in country to welcome the principal and handle security while he or she is there; meanwhile, the first agent moves on to the next stop on the itinerary to do advance work there.

Executive protection agents can be either full-time employees of the corporation or embedded from a specialist partner. Embedding agents from a partner has the advantage of trying out different agents to find those with the best fit with the corporate culture and principal. This can be a significant plus: despite all efforts to match the right people to the right jobs, the only way to really discover whether chemistry and personalities work well together in this people business is to try it out. If the corporation has to recruit, hire and fire to find the right people, this takes time and money that can be saved by drawing on a partner's deep bench.

Protective intelligence agent*

We believe that after the manager and at least two protective agents, the next full-time staff should be an intelligence agent.

Why? Because an outdated, stale RTVA can be worse than no RTVA. Basing current protection on old intelligence can easily give a false impression that the team is shaping its protective efforts according to a true picture of the principal's prominence and its resultant risks, when in fact it is not.

The protective intelligence agent is charged with ongoing updates of the RTVA, which is critical to stay on top of the changing risk and threat scenarios that impact the corporation and the principal. In addition to these updates, the intelligence agent may also be tasked with preparing regular reports on other security-related issues important to the company, or with writing ad hoc reports for destinations on the principal's itinerary.

The intelligence agent may be hired directly by the corporation or embedded. Embedding the agent from a specialist partner lets him or her draw on the partner's entire worldwide network as well as on the corporation's own resources.

Residential agents

Depending on the nature of the threats to the principal and his or her family, residential security will often also be part of the security package.

While residential security is sometimes organized separately from corporate executive protection, there are good reasons to integrate the two efforts into one program. This provides seamless coverage based on the same intelligence, managed by the same people, according to the same principles.

As described in Chapter 9, the skills and experience requirements for residential agents are lower than those for executive protection agents. In our experience, working with residential agents can provide managers with a kind of recruitment pool for executive protection positions: this gives managers a chance to see agents in action, then handpick some of them for further training and other roles.

Security drivers

Like residential agents, security drivers may or may not be integrated members of the permanent executive protection team.

When the program requires frequent use of a trained driver in the same location, for example to handle commutes between the principal's primary residence and workplace, then it often makes good organizational, protective and economic sense to retain a dedicated person for this job. Conversely, as we pointed out above, it would make no sense to hire a driver in locations that the principal visits only occasionally.

No program success without sufficient headcount

One of the easiest organizational traps to fall into, especially for new or growing programs, is insufficient staffing.

Once the manager has found and developed a handful of good agents, it can be tempting to rely on the same small cadre—even though these turn into 80-hour workweeks for the people involved. And although agents who thrive are resilient, resourceful and self-motivated, as we saw in Chapter 9, even super agents can become overworked. This reduces their operational readiness, of course, but it harms the program in other ways, too.

In the short and mid terms, relying heavily on just a few people increases the likelihood of favoritism between the principal, manager and agents. It's one thing to make sure the program respects the principal's personal preferences—also as regards the kind of agent that provides protection. But it's another thing altogether to think that only a few individuals can fill this role. Unless the team develops sufficient depth it is doomed to fail.

In the longer term, of course, this kind of work/life balance is intolerable. Even the best and most dedicated of agents will find someplace else to work.

To ensure program success, it is critical that programs be staffed realistically.

Chapter 13:
Motivating and communicating with the executive protection team

Everybody knows that communication is the lifeblood of the organization and one of the manager's most essential tasks. In fact, managers typically spend far more time communicating than on other managerial tasks such as setting objectives, organizing, following up and developing people.

If you think about it, the reasons for this are obvious. Without communicating program objectives clearly and consistently, the team won't know about them. Plans are meaningless when they stay in the manager's head. KPIs and corrective action instructions are worthless unless they are told, discussed and finally understood and internalized.

And yet survey after survey reveals that the most common employee complaint about management, across many types of organizations, is poor communication.

Although we have no statistics on the state of communication in the executive protection industry, we're quite sure they would reveal a similar tendency. On the list of what makes or breaks good corporate executive protection programs, effective communication will always be at the top.

Especially important due to what we do

Given the criticality of what we do, protecting the well-being and productivity of the corporation's top management, the importance of good communication in executive protection is only greater.

When communication breaks down—within the team, between the team and the principal, or between the team and other key stakeholders in the corporate ecosystem—program failure is just around the corner.

And when executive protection programs fail, the principal's security and efficiency are the first victims. The executive protection manager's job security could be the next.

Overcoming communication challenges in executive protection

Corporate executive protection managers face a number of particular communication challenges; it is important that they—as well as everyone else involved, including team members, principals, executive administrative assistants and others in the corporate ecosystem—be aware of them.

One set of challenges arises because the stakeholders with whom we communicate are many and varied. One day the manager may have to hammer through budget revisions in corporate finance; the next day she could be selecting agents to protect the principal's preschool daughter or giving feedback on a security driver in Nepal. Regardless, positive outcomes of all three examples depend heavily on good communication by the executive protection manager.

Another challenge occurs because team members are often scattered across time zones, and scheduling constraints can make it difficult to gather everyone in the same place. Especially in complex, 24/7/365 programs, some team members will always be on the road, at a residence or handling a detail somewhere else. They won't be in the same room, yet they need to be on the same page regarding a wide variety of issues.

But the biggest challenge is probably due to the fact that individual characteristics play such an important role in our field. Compared to other corporate endeavors, the nature of our work puts a lot of focus on team members' personalities and people skills. Whereas a prickly bookkeeper might go far in corporate finance, or an eccentric marketer could enjoy a solid career as long as her campaigns create results, executive protection agents whose temperaments strike the principal as odd will not be long in that position. Communicating directly and often about issues that are closely related to a colleague's psychological makeup is by no means easy; but it is always important in corporate executive protection management.

The hallmarks of good communication for corporate executive protection managers

Because of the special nature of what we do, executive protection managers need to take a special approach to communication. We outline below some key characteristics of good communication in executive protection programs that need constant managerial focus—and the understanding of all stakeholders:

123

- **360-degree:** As we pointed out in Chapter 4, executive protection managers need to ensure good relationships throughout the corporate ecosystem. This includes the principal and his or her executive administrative assistant, of course, but also many other corporate departments and even family offices and residential staff. It also includes everyone on the protection team, no matter where or when they work.

  Executive protection managers need to make 360-degree communication a priority. This means regular meetings, phone calls and reports; it also means making the most of each and every touch point that presents itself, whether it's a quick conversation between details or popping into someone's office when the opportunity arises.

  Of course, some stakeholders are more important than others and should be prioritized. But it must also be a priority to make the rounds.

- **Proactive:** Executive protection managers cannot afford the luxury of waiting to see what happens and then coming up with a plan. They need to think ahead, look around the corner, and be prepared for a range of eventualities before they materialize. The same holds true in communication.

  It helps the executive protection manager to think proactively in all things communicative. Through regular dialogue with the executive administrative assistant, for example, the manager is always keen to discover issues while they are still small and fixable. What happened this week? What's happening next week? Why? How are we doing, and is there anything that we can do better?

  We tell our managers that we always want the executive administrative assistant's folder to be empty. This means they must tackle issues as soon as they arise, and never let minor irritations build into major problems. This can only happen through proactive communication.

- **Immediately responsive:** When an executive protection manager discovers something that needs attention, it's important to respond quickly.

This is due not least to the criticality of what we do: when the well-being of the principal we are assigned to protect is concerned, postponing communication to a more convenient or comfortable time is not an option. We need to act on available information now, not save it for a yearly performance review.

Responsiveness is also necessitated by the personal nature of what we do. If the principal signals dissatisfaction with a team member, for example, it's better to act now than later: a quick coaching session might nip the problem in the bud. And if a personnel issue has already grown beyond repair, it's up to the manager to take decisive action, and quickly communicate this, even though the message is not a pleasant one.

- **Direct:** There can be no beating around the bush when it comes to management communication in executive protection programs. Goals and expectation need to be crystal clear to all involved. Changing SOPs must be expressed with absolute precision and without ambiguity. The same holds true for explaining and clarifying the needs of the client to staff members.

Being brutally honest does not have to mean being brutal, however. While direct communication that protects program integrity always takes precedence above other matters, it does matter that the manager treats everyone with civility. It is possible to be both completely honest and direct in one's communication, and to do so with respect and empathy. In fact, it is absolutely necessary to achieve a well-run protection program.

- **Continual:** Managers who are good communicators never rest on their laurels and take a break from communicating.

  They treat communication as a constant priority. They include regular meetings or calls in their plans; and they always find ways to make the most of any opportunity to establish a stakeholder dialogue.

- **Across time and geographic barriers:** Communicating with the entire executive protection team means being available when and where people work. If some team members work only the graveyard shift of a residential detail, then the manager needs to make the time—and the effort—to show up and talk to people even though it's late.

  Everyone on the team needs to be acknowledged and to know that he or she is an important part of the whole. They must know that they are connected to the mother ship even though they might not see it every day, and that the manager is aware of and interested in individual performance and ready to provide support as needed.

  If team members do not feel this close connection, then there is a real risk that they will not be up to date on changes in SOPs or client requirements. The probability of them becoming complacent increases; and the likelihood of the manager discovering the resultant drop in team readiness decreases.

Chapter 14:
Measuring the performance of the corporate executive protection team

As any successful manager knows, what gets measured gets done. Corporate executive protection is no different, and developing a strong set of key performance indicators (KPIs) is essential to program success.

KPIs help the corporate executive protection manager and other stakeholders in several ways:

- **Focus:** Good KPIs keep the executive protection team focused on what matters. The emphasis should be on goals that are shared and important—i.e., the ones that define the contours of program success.

- **Diagnostics:** KPIs help management see what's working well and what needs improvement. For corporate executive protection, where people are the program's most important asset, KPIs need to track both qualitative and quantitative aspects of team performance.

- **Accountability:** When it comes to security teams, there must be no doubt about who is responsible for what. KPIs enable team members to see how they contribute—and managers to understand who is or is not performing to reach program goals.

- **Preemptive corrective action:** Ongoing evaluations allow executive protection managers to identify norms and outliers over time, so they can proactively respond to performance developments before trouble hits.

- **Transparency:** Even in successful executive protection programs, it is not uncommon to be asked, "What do you guys actually do, anyway?" KPI reporting helps demonstrate that executive protection is more like a fire department than a police department. When we're not fighting fires, we're getting better at it by practicing.

KPIs are not the same as metrics. Metrics measure individual data points, whereas KPIs are sets of quantifiable metrics that enable the executive protection manager as well as principals and other stakeholders to evaluate performance against strategic and operational goals.

Best-practice KPIs for corporate executive protection

While the KPIs for individual executive protection programs will vary according to circumstances, best practice dictates that they all share the same basic characteristics.

- **Aligned with program goals:** KPIs should always help us understand program performance compared to program goals. While any individual KPI—or its underlying metrics—will not necessarily explain program success or failure, a good KPI report will let us understand whether the executive protection program is meeting its stated objectives—and to what extent.

- **Important:** You don't need to measure everything, just the important things. But sometimes important KPIs are made up of multiple metrics, none of which seems too significant in and of itself. For example, knowing how many hours team members spend on travel might not appear that critical, but the data can enable decisions on hiring remote staff and reduce overall program costs— as well as improve readiness. Similarly, because it is vital to monitor risk factors that can affect the principal's safety, correlations that affect prominence—for example, increased media exposure through planned PR activities—may be meaningful, as are travel days in emerging markets.

- **Understandable:** It might seem obvious, but we've seen enough examples to the contrary that we want to point out that KPIs must be understandable for all involved. Security professionals have a tendency to rely on jargon and acronyms that corporate stakeholders might find difficult to comprehend. Be sure to translate tactical speak into transparent KPIs.

- **Measureable**: KPIs must of course be based on measurable data. In a people business like ours, however, we should not shy away from personal evaluations that hard-nosed accountants might sneer at. KPIs for corporate executive protection can be qualitative as well as quantitative.

- **Consistent**: Over time, KPI reports let us understand developments and trends that might otherwise be difficult to spot. To be sure we are comparing apples to apples, the underlying data should be collected and correlated in a consistent way.

- **Timely**: Some things need to get evaluated sooner rather than later in order to provide value. For example, a KPI review after every detail lets us learn lessons that can be applied immediately.

Don't forget to keep track of team morale and cultural fit

Executive protection is a team effort, so evaluating the executive protection team's cohesiveness and ability to work together is important. Here are some things to consider for ongoing evaluation:

- **Shared sense of purpose:** The executive protection team and key stakeholders must clearly understand the risks and threats to principals—and the benefits of mitigating those risks in a way that enhances productivity. The executive protection team must be seen as a valuable partner in supporting the safety, satisfaction and productivity of identified principals.

- **Shared sense of team standards and approach:** It is essential that the team understand and use transparent operational standards for everything from simple scheduling to crisis procedures.

- **Good relationships and communication:** Frictionless interactions within the team and between the team and key stakeholders are essential to program success. Though not as simple to capture as other metrics, KPIs should nonetheless be developed in order to evaluate how executive protection team members cooperate with each other and relevant corporate departments and personnel.

- **Good program fit with the principal's personal preferences and corporate culture:** When executive protection teams achieve excellence, their presence is effective but unobtrusive. They facilitate productivity and security without being asked to do so, and often without being noticed; they never make the principal think twice or miss a beat, but rather adjust to the corporate culture and the principal's lifestyle.

- **Excellent team morale and readiness:** It is common—and potentially disastrous—for executive protection teams to grow complacent. If nothing happens to the principal, that can easily be confused with program success. That is why it is essential to develop KPIs that track team members' morale and operational readiness.

Potential KPI areas for corporate executive protection

There is no one-size-fits-all KPI list for corporate executive protection. Your ideal set will depend on whether your program is in start-up, turnaround or sustain mode as well as specific program objectives. Nonetheless, see below for a number of factors that will be relevant for many programs, and around which KPIs may be developed.

- Ongoing risk assessment

    — Principal prominence

    — Travel destination risks

    — Intel including social media monitoring,

    — Persons of interest

- Key stakeholder satisfaction

    — Principal/traveler feedback

    — Principal productivity

- — Key partner feedback (executive admins, corporate security, estate management, etc.)

- — Program/vendor management feedback

- — Event manager feedback

- Responsiveness

  - — Availability and appropriateness of executive protection resources

  - — Issues addressed thoroughly and quickly

  - — Short-notice request performance

- Quality of services provided

  - — Program management/organization

  - — Deliverables

  - — On-ground support (agents and transportation)

  - — Administrative activities

- Team workload

  - — Travel days

  - — Domestic trips

  - — International trips

  - — Comp time

- Readiness

  - — Training

  - — Drills

  - — Fitness evaluation

- Quality of communications

- — Appropriate

- — Accurate

- — Clear and concise

- Operational transparency

  - — Execution to expectations

  - — Clear understanding of executive protection program by key stakeholders

- Financial performance

  - — Budget expectations set and met—good financial stewardship

  - — Responsiveness to identified issues

Chapter 15:
Developing people on the corporate executive protection team

It's been true for generations, and it's especially resonant with Generation Y, the so-called Millennials born between the early '80s and '00s, who are now embarking on their careers: money motivates, of course, but the opportunity to learn and grow professionally is what really turns a wage earner into a passionate and dedicated team member.

People who are not developing in their jobs feel like they're treading water instead of making career progress. The good ones will move on to find somewhere where they can learn more and take on more responsibility. The less talented will stay on— and these are not the people we want to depend on to keep our principals safe, happy and productive.

What does this mean for corporate executive protection managers? Plenty.

If managers don't develop talent, they lose it

If those responsible for corporate executive protection don't help their staff develop and learn, then they don't deserve to be called managers. For in addition to all of the other responsibilities that fall upon them, spotting and nurturing talent is an absolutely essential cornerstone of a sustainable executive protection program.

When managers own this responsibility and dedicate serious effort to it, good things happen. The best talent will naturally gravitate to their programs. Team motivation and performance will be reliably high. Staff turnover will be predictably low.

But when managers prove unwilling to or incapable of developing people, the opposite will occur. Talent will seep away, often citing "I got a better offer at another company" as the reason. Of course, these people are smart enough not to burn their bridges to a former employer, so they would never tell HR the truth at their exit interviews: they're moving on because their manager failed to take their developmental needs seriously and didn't help them learn new skills or grow into new responsibilities.

Keeping perishable skills fresh through training

As we saw in Chapter 9, there are a number of skills that protection personnel need to possess because they are vitally important to our overall goal: mitigating risk to the principal to an acceptable level. These include basic and advanced executive protection skills, security driving and first aid.

Fortunately, of course, agents rarely if ever need to call on skills such as operating a heart defibrillator or engaging in evasive driving. This doesn't mean these skills are unimportant or irrelevant, however. Executive protection managers and HR departments need to realize that these are all perishable skills. If agents don't use them, they lose them.

That is why regular training schedules need to be developed for all teams and all agents. Some of this training will be off-site at dedicated facilities and with specialized instructors. Some of it will take place around a conference table at departmental meetings, and be conducted by the manager or a team member with subject matter expertise. All of it is important.

More than once, we've run into corporate HR departments who roll their eyes at our requirements to keep something as essential as security driving skills up to date. Didn't the agent just do that 18 months ago? Isn't zipping around a racetrack at high speed more fun than necessary? When has anything ever happened while the principal was being driven around town?

These are all reasonable questions for people with no experience in executive protection. In these cases and many others, the manager needs to step up and explain the importance of ongoing training both to develop and retain the best talent and to meet the program's goals of protecting the principal.

The importance of clear career paths

Career development planning has been a staple of other corporate departments for decades. Now, security and HR directors are finally waking up to the fact that executive protection programs also rely on professionals who pursue career opportunities—if not here, then somewhere else where they are more readily available.

As our industry develops and more and more corporations begin to implement executive protection programs, the importance of clearly defined career development plans continues to grow—albeit from a woefully low base. Far too many agents stay in the same jobs for far too long without developing new skills or increasing their level of responsibility. If we do not improve, we will soon see bottlenecks as more companies require good executive protection managers but find it difficult to fill the positions.

The bad news is that it's necessary even to raise this issue. As an industry, we have been far too haphazard in how we develop people as part of professionalizing our services. Corporations have relied on retired law enforcement officers or military veterans whose careers were more in sunset than start-up mode; along with them, dedicated executive protection firms have not done enough to improve career planning and development. This has to change.

The good news is that we don't need to reinvent the wheel to bring on significant improvements. We can start by borrowing tried-and-true methods honed by corporate HR departments the world over, such as systems for spotting and nurturing high performance employees, formalized career development plans for everyone, improved coaching and mentoring skills for managers, and aligning job classifications, salaries and benefits against clearly defined career milestones.

Informal versus formal learning...

Now, it might be tempting simply to bring in some HR consultants to set up a formalized system of training and career development for executive protection programs, throw some money at them, then sit back to wait for results. Sorry, but while this might all help, it is far from sufficient.

As everyone except training companies knows, "informal" learning is what really enables people to acquire new skills and improve their performance at work. The single largest driver is experience, of course: we learn best by doing.

The most important knowledge and skills that we need to perform in a job are acquired on the job in communities of practice. We look and learn from others, we call on people in our network to explain how things work, and we naturally gravitate to those subject matter experts who are generous with their expertise.

Does this mean that the executive protection manager doesn't need to do anything special to ensure that people learn on the job? Hardly.

...and the role of the executive protection manager

Executive protection managers are instrumental in enabling both the formalized training and the informal learning that enables staff to learn and grow. If they aren't living and breathing this responsibility every day, they aren't doing their jobs.

Good managers seize every chance to create learning and development opportunities. Instead of saving everything for a yearly review, they'll make use of even a little downtime to learn more about their staff's developmental interests and career goals.

Once a detail is completed and it's time for an after-action review, they'll ask simple questions like "What are the lessons learned?" When they plan a new detail they'll consider—and inquire into—how individual agents can contribute and what they'd like to learn. What would it take to bump the person up a notch in terms of responsibility?

The learning-oriented manager always makes it a point to keep everyone on the team informed of the big picture. What's going on in the organization that can impact our work? Where are the best practices that can inspire us to do better? How are others embodying the values that we want to inform our work?

As executive protection managers, we need to take learning and development seriously.

Think back on the teachers you had while growing up, and you'll probably remember one or two with particular fondness.

Do the same with the list of managers you've had throughout your career: some will stand out as people who have been instrumental in helping you make career progress. We've all met them. We need more of them in the executive protection industry.

Part III:
Transitions in corporate executive protection

Introduction to Part III: Change management in corporate EP: start-up, turnaround, realign or sustain?

As in all other matters, changes in corporate EP programs are inevitable. For as Lao Tzu noted centuries ago, "If you do not change direction, you may end up where you are heading." And that's not always where you actually want to go.

So for those of us involved in managing corporate EP programs, understanding the challenges that organizations face at the various pivot points of EP programs is crucial.

Now, in Part III of this book, we examine the key transitions that corporate EP programs are likely to face at one time or another. Our focus is on the first two transitional phases—start-up and turnaround—as these are the most relevant for most companies.

To do so, we borrow from Michael Watkins of Harvard Business School, who has written extensively on managing business and career transitions. He provides some great, actionable insights that can also be applied to corporate EP programs by chief security officers, EP managers and corporate boards—not to mention principals.

We've taken the liberty of tweaking Watkins's five-pointed STAR model down to the four transitions that are most relevant for corporate EP programs:

- Start-up

- Turnaround

- Realignment

- Sustaining success

For those tasked with managing corporate EP programs, much of Watkins's solid advice holds true across all four transitions. This includes the necessity of aligning program changes with (corporate EP) strategy, understanding the corporation's cultural and political environments, relentless focus on key priorities, creating supportive alliances and the importance of early wins.

While the long-term goals of the corporate EP program—keeping principals safe, happy and productive—do stand up to the test of time, short-term goals will vary according to which transition phase the program is in. Let's take a closer look at these four transitions.

Chapter 16:
Starting up a corporate executive protection program

Every corporate executive protection program starts somewhere. And although a number of Fortune 500 and other companies already use executive protection, a significant segment still does not. Navigating the start-up phase of a corporate executive protection program is particularly tricky for many chief security officers, boards and would-be principals: They're simply not familiar with executive protection, and they're starting from scratch.

The transition

This chapter address the process of moving from no executive protection program to a working program—even at a small scale. The addition of a second principal to an existing program can in many ways also be considered a start-up, as can succession from one CEO to another.

Key objectives

Get an executive protection program running where there has been none, or get an executive protection program running for a new principal.

Key milestones

1. Bringing about the realization that a professional executive protection program is necessary, feasible and a sound investment

2. Gathering the capabilities and defining the processes that will make it happen

3. Delivering a first impression of operational excellence—even if this is more of a "baby step" than a giant leap forward

Key challenges

- **Lack of experience with corporate executive protection:** The corporation has no expertise or track record in executive protection, no "this is how we usually do it," and normally no one on board with any practical executive protection insight.

   What is more, preconceived notions and misconceptions abound. Although a CSO might have a clear idea about the differences between professional executive protection and "bodyguards," the principal and most of the board probably won't. Understandably, most executives with no executive protection experience will easily confuse the tabloid image of intrusive bodyguards with the reality of well-trained executive protection agents. They will quickly pull up the same pictures of close protection as the general population: Hollywood stars walking behind a phalanx of muscle-bound men in black; scruff-ups with paparazzi; insensitive indiscretions and tell-all book deals.

That means the most important barrier to initiating a corporate executive protection program is ignorance of what executive protection actually is (and isn't).

It is often the case that everyone involved in a new corporate executive protection program will have to reassess their conception of executive protection. So one of our most important tasks in the start-up phase is establishing clarity about the nature of a professional executive protection program and its actual value. This has direct communication consequences for a wide range of C-level players, starting with the principal, board and CSO. As we discussed in Chapter 4, however, we need to collaborate and communicate with many other stakeholders throughout the organization.

- **Building the corporate executive protection network from scratch:** A brand-new executive protection program will have no established network to rely on, so every connection to every stakeholder will have to be created and nurtured. Let's look at just a few of the departments with which a new program will need to build strong bridges of mutual understanding in order to overcome a lack of experience with corporate executive protection.

  — **Finance needs to deal with unpredictable costs:** Executive protection finances are often different than those of other corporate departments. Among other things, everyone from accounts payable to the CFO will need to understand the vagaries of executive protection budgeting: When the CEO decides to take an unplanned trip in the middle of a budget year, the variable costs of executive protection advance planning, travel and manpower shoot up with every new itinerary.

— **HR needs to hire a new kind of employee:** Corporate executive protection programs may also send HR departments on a steep learning curve. If the program includes insourcing executive protection agents and/or a manager, HR departments will need to hire, develop and remunerate entirely different kinds of employees than those essential to their core businesses. It should be noted that those who view executive protection manager and agent positions as easy "retirement jobs" for most military veterans or former law enforcement officers do so at their peril. HR recruiters need to realize that these are specialist roles best filled by qualified candidates.

Staffing levels must be correct from the start or soon become so. Applying corporate cookie-cutter staffing policies and procedures to executive protection agents who might be called on to work 80-hour weeks and spend more time on the road than at home will have its own consequences.

Another HR issue is training: Even well-trained executive protection agents are only as good as their readiness, and readiness depends on constantly keeping complacency at bay. Some executive protection skills are perishable, and while HR departments new to executive protection may find courses in, for example, emergency driving, more "nice to have" than "need to have," this unfamiliarity with executive protection best practices should not be allowed to impinge on the program's overall effectiveness.

- **Executive administrative assistants add a new stakeholder:** A good executive protection program depends on close cooperation with the executive administrative assistant (EAA). EAAs need to see executive protection personnel as partners, not competitors; executive protection managers need to see EAAs as more than gatekeepers.

- **CSO anxiety:** Most chief security officers have little or no practical experience with setting up or running a corporate executive protection program, and thus face particular challenges.

  One thing is sure: All eyes will be on the new executive protection program; all services will be examined critically—especially during the initial phases of the start-up. For the CSO, the stakes can seem daunting. There are risks, and although the potential rewards are high if the program succeeds, so are the repercussions in case of program failure.

- **Navigating new territory without a map:** Since executive protection is a relatively new component of many corporate security programs, CSOs have no established patterns to follow. Standard best practices are not known; benchmarking with industry leaders is difficult; make-buy decisions regarding program setup are unclear.

- **Conflicting interests:** It is not uncommon that the corporation's board of directors mandates an EP program for a CEO—even though the principal perceives no need for executive protection and has no desire to be any part of it. As we learned in Chapter 3, corporate boards have their own reasons for mandating executive protection programs; these may or may not be aligned with the principal or his/her immediate staff. In the case of executive protection, it is the CSO's job to make everyone happy—or at least to minimize dissatisfaction—and that may include navigating between interests apparently at odds with each other.

- **CEO scrutiny:** The results of the CSO's work on a new executive protection program suddenly become very visible, significant and personal for a CEO with whom he may not otherwise have much interaction. While few CEOs dig into the minutiae of campus security guards or biometric door locks, you can be sure that all will have an opinion on an executive protection program and executive protection agents. These opinions are quickly directed to the CSO responsible for the executive protection program.

- **Complex reporting lines:** Even in convoluted matrix organizations, employees are seldom in doubt as to "who is the boss." Corporate executive protection is a little different. Most CEOs will defer to the chain of command if they notice a lower-level company employee who needs to be nudged, reprimanded or ultimately replaced. But if the principal doesn't like an executive protection agent—for whatever reason—personal preferences trump corporate hierarchy every time. Similarly, if the CEO's assistant lets the executive protection manager know that a sudden, unbudgeted trip has come up, there is probably no time for special procedures to exceed agreed budgets. Dotted lines become stronger than solid lines in an instant, and CSOs need to take responsibility for the whole show.

Important early wins

In light of the challenges we briefly discuss above, a few initial victories emerge clearly for those who are tasked with starting up a corporate EP program from scratch.

- **Acceptance of the need for executive protection:** The first must-win battle is gaining approval from the board and principal to provide at least *some* executive protection services somewhere, some time. It often makes good sense to commence an executive protection program with "baby steps" rather than a full-blown, 24/7/365 program. This gives everyone involved the opportunity to experience firsthand what professional executive protection actually is. If done properly, it also makes clear that corporate executive protection provides all-important collateral benefits: improved travel logistics and increased productivity.

- **Operational excellence:** First impressions matter. Another must-win battle is that of executive protection quality. It is essential that the principal and the rest of the organization meet only well trained and carefully selected executive protection agents—always, of course, and *especially* in the early days of the program. While the program might able to survive a less-than-optimal executive protection agent after running for a while, if the principal's and organization's initial perceptions of program quality are negative, it might be too late to fix the reputation of a program that got off to a bad start.

- **Relationship building:** Creating bridges rather than walls between key stakeholders in the organization is critical, for without these the executive protection program will flounder. To build relationships in a start-up program, executive protection professionals must realize that they have a double role: Not only must they execute their jobs flawlessly, but they must also develop stakeholder understanding of what good executive protection is and how it happens. This will involve a lot of explaining and, not least, relentlessly demonstrating a professional executive protection approach throughout the corporate executive protection ecosystem.

Chapter 17:
Turning around a corporate executive protection program that is in trouble

Considering the many challenges of starting up a corporate executive protection program, it's no wonder that some are more successful than others. Some programs never get off the ground in the right way, and some become outright failures. A company and its principal might come to the conclusion that executive protection is not for them.

In most cases, however, just because a company's current executive protection program is not performing as expected or wished does not mean that its underlying objective—the principal's safety, productivity and happiness—is no longer a priority. Rather than simply terminating the program, what's called for is a turnaround.

The transition

Moving from a dysfunctional or unsatisfactory executive protection program to one that works—and ideally keeps the principal and other key stakeholders happy.

Key objectives

Turn a non-performing executive protection program into a high-performing program.

Key milestones

1. Recognition that the executive protection program is non-performing.

2. Correct assessment of the root causes of the problem(s)

3. Creating a turnaround plan that prioritizes key issues and improvement steps

4. Focus on early wins

Key challenges

- **Awareness:** The first hurdle to overcome in a turnaround situation is recognizing the need for change. Moving people beyond denial to realize that there are problems—and that change is needed to correct these—is imperative.

   This is not just a question of checking some simple metrics. A poorly functioning executive protection program will probably not have a clear way to evaluate success or failure, and unlike other managers, those responsible for executive protection may have difficulty in rallying the troops around an obvious gap analysis. That means they will need to use something else.

   A SWOT analysis of the program with focus on problem assessment is essential. Given the personal nature of many executive protection activities, it may often be more effective to bring in third-party expertise to conduct these analyses than to expect that those responsible for creating the situation will also have the wherewithal to rectify it.

Another challenge can be creating consensus around the problem analysis and the root causes of the problems. It is essential that the CSO, principal and executive protection manager get on the same page before deciding to turn a new leaf.

- **Prioritizing the most critical pain points:** Since a dysfunctional program may suffer from a long list of troubles, it can be tempting to try to address all of them at once. This is not a good idea.

The turnaround process can be compared to medical triage: Among many wounds and illnesses, we have to assign a degree of urgency to and address all issues in the optimal sequence. First stop the bleeding, then start the breathing, protect the wound and treat for shock. Identify the roots of the trouble, then address these aggressively.

It is better to hone in on the most critical reasons for the problems and to then focus on these relentlessly throughout the turnaround. The turnaround plan should build on addressing these few core problems, and early wins should hinge on ameliorating their root causes.

- **Stabilization:** In most cases, the program must go on even while analysis of its problems is taking place: Dropping protection of the principal is not an option. Stabilizing a program while preparing to change it may bring challenges of its own.

- **Creating a vision for the future:** In order to be successful, those responsible for the turnaround must paint a clear picture of how the new executive protection program will look once the root causes of underperformance have been identified and corrected. Giving people a realistic image of the light at the end of the tunnel allows them to embrace a shared vision—and to look forward rather than backward.

  It is important that the vision be clear and compelling—but not so detailed that the turnaround team paints itself into a corner that may be difficult to get out of as the process continues. Creating unrealistic expectations impinges on credibility—see below.

- **Building credibility:** The program's reputation within the corporation is all-important, and trust in an executive protection program is one of the hardest things to rebuild once it has been undermined by poor performance. Therefore, managing expectations through thoughtful communication is essential in all executive protection turnarounds.

  Transparency around the turnaround process is important, and those tasked with the turnaround should be as open as possible. If there is bad news, it should all be broken at once rather than rationing it across weeks or months. New teams have the privilege of starting with a fresh slate: They can acknowledge current and past shortcomings, set a new direction, and move on.

  Of course, the new team must make good on its promises in order to build its own credibility. By communicating goals you know you can achieve—and meeting them—executive protection managers build confidence and put precious credit into the emerging program's reliability account.

Important early wins

- **Creating consensus on the turnaround plan:** Once your analysis is complete, you need to be sure that all key stakeholders are on the same page as to what the core problems are and how the turnaround plan will correct these. Key stakeholders will typically include the principal, the CSO and perhaps the executive protection manager if there is one.

- **Reorganizing for success:** If your analysis reveals that there is a person or persons who are standing in the way of a successful executive protection turnaround—or who is largely responsible for the program's dismal state—then you should consider moving quickly to remove these people from the team. This could be one or more executive protection agents or even the executive protection manager. Although it's a difficult thing to do, if your analysis indicates that someone is more part of the problem than of the solution, then they should not be allowed to stand in the way of the turnaround. Furthermore, by reorganizing early on, you send the signal that you are willing to make changes—also the tougher ones.

- **Reporting using relevant metrics:** Since your turnaround efforts will be using metrics that are directly related to the pain points that the turnaround is designed to address, it is good idea to begin reporting against these metrics.

The importance of keeping up turnaround momentum

There is a tendency for the people involved in an executive protection turnaround to think that they have completed their job once the program is out of immediate trouble. It's natural to celebrate the pain being over, but the festivities shouldn't last too long.

Even though it's easy to overlook or choose not to deal with other underlying issues which might later disrupt the program, smart managers will keep the turnaround going until all concerns have been faced and dealt with.

They won't get trapped by the arrogance that their program is so good that it does not need any adjustments. They will root out bad habits and poor results even if they aren't causing immediate pain. They'll be aware of other problems such as favoritism, complacency and lack of focus on improvement.

Chapter 18:
Realigning a corporate executive program that needs to change course

Sometimes an executive protection program might seem to be running fine at the present moment, but still be headed for trouble. Unlike a turnaround situation where the program is clearly in crisis, an executive protection program in need of realignment may not be marked by obvious signals of distress or urgency for change.

Another situation that we sometimes see, especially in post-turnaround programs, is also a sign that realignments are in order. After having fixed a program's most critical pain points, there is a tendency to think the program is out of trouble, and it's tempting to rest on your laurels. But just because a program's weakest elements have been strengthened, this doesn't mean the program is as good as it can be. Good CSOs and executive protection managers will continue to push for improvements to make sure the program is always performing at its very best.

The challenges of a realignment transition make up a kind of middle ground between a turnaround and sustaining a successful program. Some program elements work well; others do not. Nonetheless, the careful observer will see clouds gathering on the horizon and realize that if the program sticks to its present course, significant problems will be inevitable.

If a successful program begins to slip, a realignment could head off the need for a turnaround. If the realignment fails, however, then program turnaround will be the only alternative.

The transition

Make changes in a program in order to readjust the executive protection strategy, deliveries and culture, and thus bolster program quality in the face of anticipated challenges.

Key objectives

Ensure continued program success in spite of predictable factors that will make this more difficult; revitalize a program that is headed for trouble.

Key milestones

1. Building consensus for the need for change
2. Realignment plan with concrete steps
3. Restructuring as needed

Key challenges

- **Complacency:** If nothing ever happens to the principal (and fortunately, it rarely does) and he or she seems fairly happy, then it can be tempting to assume that the executive protection program is performing well. Tempting, but potentially misguided: The program's underlying strategy, culture and operations might all be in need of an overhaul, and the principal's well-being heretofore may well be as much a product of chance as of the executive protection program's design and execution.

Readiness declines with complacency. Maintaining an alert executive protection program that responds to changing risks, needs and environments requires constant management attention.

- **Outdated executive protection strategy:** Executive protection strategies need to be critically reviewed from time to time. One reason: An RTVA that is years old is likely outdated and no longer useful. An executive protection strategy that has remained unchanged in the face of organizational, technological or market developments is probably no longer serving its original purpose.

  Like other business areas, there is no reason to create a new executive protection strategy every year. But ongoing RTVA updates and periodic strategy audits should inform all realignment processes.

- **Program culture:** Over time, all corporate executive protection programs will develop their own culture or sub-culture. A healthy culture will be characterized by openness, consistent dedication to improvement and the ability to learn from mistakes, resilience in the face of difficulties and a high degree of personal accountability—just to mention a few attributes. Unhealthy cultures—well, that's the stuff of another book. Suffice it to say that entrenched ways of doing things and unspoken rules can be a barrier—as well as a support—to realigning an executive protection culture and program that needs to change.

- **Favoritism:** One thing we will mention about unhealthy executive protection cultures is favoritism. We all want to be liked, and some of us may be more likeable than others in a given situation. But a good corporate executive protection team does not allow favoritism to get in the way of professionalism. When some relationships between executive protection agents and the principal get cozier than others, that's a sure sign of trouble.

- **Skills gap:** An executive protection team that does not have the skills it needs to perform at a high level is one thing. This can addressed by training, new hires, outsourcing or other means—and is indeed often is part of a realignment strategy.

  But an executive protection program in need of realignment could well be in the situation where stakeholders simply don't possess the means of properly auditing and rectifying executive protection performance. While internal or external management consultants could be a valuable resource in other corporate realignment processes, the special nature of executive protection usually means that the corporation will not have the knowhow to effectively improve executive protection programs on its own.

Important early wins

- **Acknowledging the need for change:** The most important early win in a realignment transition is making key stakeholders aware that the status quo is not a sustainable option. Without a burning platform this can be difficult to achieve, but unless this new awareness forms the basis of the realignment effort, it will be doomed to failure.

- **Tangible changes that are in line with the realignment diagnosis:** Programs in need of realignment have strengths as well as weaknesses. Managers should aim for clear changes, early on, that make the strong stronger and the weak weaker.

Organizationally, this could mean promoting someone who displays the kind of behavior called for by the new strategy, or demoting or removing someone who does not prove to be willing or able to do so.

In terms of policy, tangible changes could reflect new priorities on readiness and training, advance planning or practically any other aspect of the program. It all depends on the situation

Chapter 19:
Sustaining high performance in a successful corporate executive protection program

It may seem counterintuitive, but even excellent executive protection programs must be challenged to change in order to stay successful. The best way to do this is to make continuous improvement a cornerstone of the corporation's executive protection program and culture.

Unlike the other program transitions described above, changes brought on by continuous improvement efforts are likely to be incremental, not revolutionary. Continuous improvement goals should be pursued throughout the program—

not only in a few parts of it—and they should be focused on personnel as well as processes and innovation.

The transition

Continuous, incremental quality improvements for the entire executive protection program are a kind of gradual transition, whereas succession of a successful and respected program leader may be more abrupt.

Key objectives

Keep a high-performing executive protection program on track—and make it even better.

Key milestones

1. Roadmap to structure all continuous improvement processes

2. Creating and using clear metrics that are based on common understanding, measuring cultural alignment as well as performance

Key challenges

- **Developing a high-performance culture:** Executive protection programs with high-performance cultures are easy to recognize but hard to copy. High-performance teams and organizations have cultures to match, and often share a number of characteristics. These include:

  — Excellent leadership aligned with the overall organization

  — No-fat organizational structure with clear roles and responsibilities

— Ongoing motivation of the organization's engagement in excellence and readiness to change

— A strong HR strategy that focuses on recruiting the very best talent for every role, then developing it even further

- **Comparative analysis and benchmarking:** It's always possible to learn from the best in the field, and benchmarking your program with high performers is an excellent way to do it.

Within the specialized niche of corporate executive protection, however, this is not as easy to do as in other areas. But it is still possible. One way to do it is to network with other CSOs and executive protection managers; another is to hire a third-party provider with a proven track record of excellence in corporate executive protection to perform a comparative review.

Important ongoing wins

The wins we want in sustaining successful programs are continuous and will typically be baked into the program itself.

Remember, success breeds success...until it doesn't. Never get complacent!

No matter what transition is the next one for your executive protection program, one thing is sure: You are never better than your last detail. So step up and never step down. Constant focus on quality deliveries should always be an objective for the entire team as they rise above self-limiting behavior to meet the ever-changing challenges of corporate executive protection.

Conclusion:
The future of corporate executive protection

As the Danish cartoonist Storm P wrote, it's difficult to make predictions—especially about the future.

We will nonetheless take a stab at this in the final chapter of our book. Not because we can be sure in our prognostications, of course, but because we firmly believe that forward thinking helps provide good security—and will also contribute to improving the entire executive protection industry.

Professionalization and consolidation will continue to shape the executive protection industry

As specialist partners professionalize their services and operations to keep up with the growing requirements of international corporate clients, we expect the executive protection industry to mature even more in the next 10 years—and at a much faster pace than during the last 10 years.

As in other relatively fragmented industries, Mom and Pop companies continue to have a disproportionate share of the corporate executive protection market. Security companies that service shopping malls and banks are still in some cases called on to provide close personal protection for corporate clients.

We believe this will change as we see more consolidation throughout the entire industry. Specialist partner security firms who are able to serve major corporations will grow in expertise as well as market share, and smaller firms will either give up or experience flat growth.

The focus on quality executive protection will increase

Corporations' focus on the quality of their executive protection programs—and thus on the qualifications of the agents and managers that provide them—will only increase in the future, we expect.

The role of the executive protection manager will be even more in focus. And for managers as well as agents, more emphasis will be placed on soft skills, training and actual corporate executive protection experience, and less on simply having a background in law enforcement or the military.

Corporations will place more importance on executive protection's business value

At some point soon, the term "executive protection" might be due for an overhaul. A more descriptive name for what we actually do (albeit not as easy to say) would be "executive protection and productivity enhancement."

We have known for a long time that good corporate executive protection must do more than mitigate risk. It must also enable the principal to get more done in less time. Smooth travel logistics allow "the highest paid person in the room" to be in more rooms in more places, get there with less stress and be as productive on the road as at home.

We believe that is why more and more boards will put a pencil to the business value of best-in-class executive protection programs. In addition to duty of care toward highly prominent execs and protecting shareholder value, enabling better productivity is good for C-suite principals and good for business. Everything else being equal, it even creates competitive advantage.

Executive protection programs will be more thoroughly integrated in the corporate organization

Planning that integrates executive protection into overall corporate strategies, values and culture will be more commonplace. More chief security officers will consider it to be an integral part of their overall area of responsibility.

Better performance management and ongoing quality improvement programs will play an increasingly vital role on the HR side. Even finance departments will be more involved as cost drivers become more transparent.

As globalization increases, the need for secure travel logistics will grow even more...

As globalization increases, more companies will be looking for more protection in more places.

This trend will only be reinforced by other forces such as increasing focus on disparity of income and the internet's insatiable thirst for celebrity stories. The prominence of high net worth and ultra-high net worth individuals and their families will increase, creating the need for better understanding of the consequent risks, threats and vulnerabilities—and how to mitigate them.

But we predict that requirements for secure travel will increase not only for members of the C-suite. Lower-level execs, service technicians and others will also be provided with more travel support. Travel, HR and legal departments will consider duty of care obligations alongside growth opportunities in unfamiliar territories—and this will be reflected in more decisions to mitigate predictable risks for travelers and expats.

...and we will see more executive protection in emerging markets

As we grow older in many OECD countries, a full 90 percent the world's population under the age of 30 live in emerging market and developing economies. The global economy's highest growth rates will continue to be found here. And by 2025, it is estimated that half of the world's Fortune 500 companies will be located in emerging markets.

This will mean a profound shift in focus for the executive protection industry. Not only will we be taking more trips to and helping more Western expats in countries throughout Africa, Asia and Latin America, but many of our customers will originate from and have their headquarters in emerging markets, so we will develop and maintain resources there to provide the protection they need.

Since the businesses of practically all of our corporate clients are inherently global, specialist executive protection partners must also have a broad international footprint. We need to be ready to serve our clients wherever they go. This, too, will mean that smaller local and regional players will often come up short when travel needs grow, further driving the consolidation trend described above.

New technology will continue to create problems as well as solutions

Practically every new technological advance in the security sphere creates opportunities as well as threats—no matter which side of the protection equation you are on.

The bad guys keep up on tech news like the rest of. Every time we start using a new piece of tech to improve security, somebody somewhere is trying to figure out a way to breach it.

One example is the "Internet of Things." Wireless security cameras have become so good and portable that they are now an integral part of our "halls and walls" surveillance on many details—also on the road. But as more and more of the things we all use, from cameras to cars to thermostats, include embedded computational devices connected to the internet, the amount of data they generate about what we do grows exponentially. Gartner estimates that as many as 26 billion "things" will be connected by 2020. The privacy and security implications are massive, and too complex to cover in this book.

Who knows what kind of new tech tools will be available in 10 years? Suffice it to say that we are already constantly upping our game, and that the future will bring even more challenges.

Intelligence analysis will become more widespread at the corporate level

Many companies already understand the value of gathering and analyzing information of all kinds to improve operational continuity and inform better business decisions. As globalization continues, the need for information that is timely, accurate and relevant—even for far-off markets—will only increase.

But dedicated intel analysts add value to corporate executive protection, too: they provide ongoing Risk, Threat and Vulnerability Assessments (RTVAs) for the principals we protect. While any executive protection program worth its salt builds on an accurate RTVA, far too many fail to update them and rely on a static evaluation even though factors affecting the principal's relative prominence—and resulting risks—change constantly. We believe this will change in the future.

There are two interesting trends regarding intelligence analysis, already occurring now, that we expect to see more of in the future.

One is that more and more companies will establish dedicated teams of in-house intel analysts rather than relying solely on off-the-shelf intelligence. These companies want to fine-tune their analyses to the organization's specific requirements. Analysts will be tasked with a broad range of projects related not only to security, but also to operations, planning, reputation management, CSR, etc.

The other interesting trend is that even though corporations want these intel resources in house, they will increasingly turn to specialist partners to get the job done. We hire, train and manage a growing number of intel analysts for our clients, then embed them within the client organization. We expect to do more of this in the future to respond to our clients' demands.

Personalization will drive more security programs

If you've read this far, you'll know that we are convinced that executive protection must adapt to the corporate culture and personal preferences of the principals we serve. We believe such personalized security services will become more prevalent in the future, and, indeed, the norm. Not because they're trendy, but because that's what actually works best.

We predict demand for highly personalized programs will only increase in the future. Clients are becoming savvier about what executive protection can be, and will be less likely to settle for plain vanilla solutions when they would actually prefer — and be better off with—something that caters specifically to their individual needs.

Appendix:
Case studies

Trip to Brazil reverses the principal's objections to executive protection

We're often approached by security directors who require protection for someone in their C-suite, but the principal wants nothing to do with executive protection.

The reasons for such resistance can be many, but typically fall into four categories: preconceived, negative notions of intrusive protection; bad previous experiences with executive protection; a conviction that executive protection is unnecessary for them; and a belief that it's too expensive and not worth the cost.

In this case, the principal had been provided with protection agents and security drivers by other companies on a number of previous trips, and had been turned off by their invasive, pushy demeanor.

The challenge: Overcoming a principal's resistance to executive protection

Our client's security director was frustrated and concerned. One of his principals was scheduled for a trip to Brazil that would include traveling to high-risk areas, but the principal had time and again refused to use any kind of executive protection, and had no intention of changing his mind for this particular trip.

The problem was that the principal had previously felt imposed upon by security agents and drivers on other trips, and the experience had left such a bad impression that he refused to acquiesce to the security department's recommendations, even though the itinerary called for it.

The security director approached us: Could AS Solution set up a security detail that would be acceptable to the principal— and still provide much-needed protection during a trip to rural Brazil?

The solution: Careful understanding of the principal's preferences, and tailor-made unobtrusive protection

We worked with the client to better understand the principal's personal preferences, and we discovered that while he recognized the need for security, he simply didn't want to see it around him. He prized his personal space and abhorred the thought of sharing it with a group of burly toughs in sunglasses. He was willing to "put up" with security only if it was all but invisible.

To meet the principal's wishes while mitigating predictable risks, our project coordinator decided on a two-pronged approach that involved people and planning. This was important, especially concerning the highest-risk elements of this particular trip, which involved travel by car through several dodgy areas.

We hand-picked the drivers and agents best suited for the job, then devised a tactical plan that placed agents in vehicles in front of and behind the principal's vehicle, but never right next to him. The security was tight, but hard to spot unless you were looking for it.

The results: A satisfied traveler who is now a regular customer

Once again, clearly articulated expectations were the first step to desired results.

By briefing the Brazilian team on the kind of people we wanted, then working with them to devise a tactical plan that respected the client's preferences, the trip went off smoothly and the principal never had reason to notice the heightened protection level.

He completed his business in Brazil without incident, and upon his return to the United States let the security director know that that was how he liked security to be provided. Since then, we have had the opportunity to serve the same principal on other trips—and to demonstrate that executive protection can only truly work when it respects the personal preferences of those we protect.

Truly personalized residential security is the only kind that really works

Residential security is important to all of us, so it's no wonder that sales of burglar alarms and other home security systems—both monitored and unmonitored—have boomed in recent years.

Unfortunately, however, many of these systems don't live up to their marketing hype. The reality is that alarms go off for no reason, or don't go off when they should. Call centers don't respond as agreed. Just look at customer service ratings for the largest home security company in the United States.

The upshot is that homeowners stop using their security systems. Even in Silicon Valley, where median home prices in some zip codes are north of $4 million, an estimated 90 percent of homes with security systems simply don't use them. The most common complaints are that they're inconvenient, don't work as expected and are ugly. Sound familiar?

The challenge: Design a home security system that matches the family's lifestyle and that they would be happy to use

Our client was building a new multimillion-dollar home with a guest annex, and his company required that the new home be equipped with a security system. He couldn't stand using the one installed in his current home, and made it clear to the architects that the new system would have to be all but invisible and work far better than the one he had.

After the architectural team tried and failed to achieve an acceptable solution with a security system integrator, they called us. Could AS Solution help design a security system for the new home that would meet the client's requirements for a customized system that was also aesthetically pleasing?

The solution: A solid understanding of the family's personal preferences—and close cooperation with architects, contractors and suppliers

We began by conducting an RTVA, which indicated that home invasion was the most significant risk, even in the upscale neighborhood where the new home was being built.

We then worked with the family to better understand their vision of the ideal security setup and their personal preferences. Where were the pain points of their current system? What were the rhythms of their day and week? How did they like to receive guests? Did they prefer to see who was at the door through a window or via a security camera? What would they do first in case they heard an alarm go off in the middle of the night?

The answers to these and many other questions enabled us to create a security concept that we first tested and refined with the family, then used as our "bible" to work closely with architects, contractors and suppliers. To strike the right balance between aesthetics, lifestyle and security some doors and windows were manufactured according to our specifications, and all security hardware was installed effectively but unobtrusively.

The results: A customized security system that the family enjoys using

Staying true to the family's lifestyle while respecting architectural ideals *and* security best practices is only possible through close cooperation, clear communication and good planning. But when all stakeholders commit to this goal from the start of the building project, rather than tacking security on at the end, successful outcomes are much more likely—as was the case here.

The family now has a highly effective security system that is designed around their lifestyle. They and their architects like that it is basically invisible. We like that it is so simple to live with and so aligned with their personal preferences that it actually gets used and serves its purpose: keeping the family safe, happy and productive while at home.

A productive trip to Morocco—in the middle of a general strike

Smooth travel logistics is one of the key building blocks of good executive protection. It enables principals to concentrate on the business rather than on the details of getting from A to B. It lets executives pack more meetings into less time and more places. And it always puts productivity front and center without ever compromising security.

While the logistical benefits of executive protection are clear even during a routine commute from home to the office, they become even more apparent on trips to emerging markets. In many of these countries, traffic accidents are still a major cause of death and injury, so the elevated risks of road travel are one reason to leave the driving to specially trained and vetted professionals. But security know-how, local knowledge and networks, and cultural and linguistic fluency also combine to facilitate trips to emerging markets in other ways, too.

The challenge: Get the principals to their meetings despite a general strike that cut off traffic to the airport

Our principals had plans to travel to Morocco when labor unions there called for a general strike of public and private sector workers. While general strikes in the North African country had only limited effect in 2014, prior to that they had created considerable unrest. The call for labor action came at a sensitive time: a string of government reforms had triggered numerous protests and tensions were high. The day of the strike happened to be the day our client had planned to arrive. To make matters worse, taxi drivers announced plans to blockade traffic to and from the airport to which our principals were arriving.

Due to scheduling constraints, however, our client was intent on carrying out the trip if possible. They contacted AS Solution to ask us to find a way to make the trip possible, despite the strike that threatened to paralyze the country.

The solution: Use local know-how and networks to determine risk, then find the path of least resistance

The first thing our operations team did was to reach out to our contacts in Morocco to get a clear picture of the situation and its risks. Our intelligence sources assured us that although the strike would create numerous inconveniences, the likelihood of any violence was low, and the itinerary our client had planned would keep them well out of harm's way.

The question of getting from the airport to the city was another matter. Cab drivers were expected to block the main roads to and from the airport in order to enforce the strike; gridlock on the usual routes was inevitable, and "scabs" who attempted to break the blockade would not be well seen. Our local Moroccan partners had good contacts throughout the city, however, and were able to select several alternative routes that would allow us to securely move the principals between the airport and meeting locations without provoking or running into any trouble.

The results: A safe, productive trip despite a difficult situation

Our client was able to complete the trip as planned and without any real inconvenience, taking care of business despite the disruptions that marked the city.

The vetted security driver we assigned to the job was a seasoned pro with excellent knowledge of local conditions and a strong network. He was able to move the principals from the airport into the city, between the hotel and meetings, and back to the airport—all as planned.

After finishing the Moroccan leg of their trip as originally scheduled, the client then moved on to the next country.

Responsive security deflates the risk of workplace violence

Workplace violence is often misunderstood. Despite the "going postal" myth, postal workers are less likely to be victims of crime than many other labor groups. Homicides and violent attacks are highly publicized but rare; other types of violence and disruption, however, are far more widespread and a drain on employee well-being and productivity. These includes threats, harassment, confrontations and other incidents that rarely make the news.

It may be tempting to think that international terrorists and career thugs pose the most serious threats to corporate executives and other employees. But thorough risk, threat and vulnerability analyses should also look inward to the possibility of trouble that originates within the company. Our experience shows that much of this can be red-flagged, then mitigated by quick preventive action.

The challenge: The threat of workplace violence thousands of miles away

Our client is a Fortune 500 conglomerate with hundreds of thousands of employees and widespread activities across the United States and abroad. The company does a large number of mergers and acquisitions each year and maintains offices in dozens of cities.

With such a large workforce spread across a variety of industries, and frequent organizational changes, the company has established procedures for dealing with the threat of workplace violence. The present case is a good example of how they handle this—and how AS Solution assists.

We received a call from them at 6:24 one morning with a request for assistance. An employee at one of their facilities in the Southeast had become a concern for the safety of management and other employees. That morning he had become emotional and turned in his badge, behaving erratically and threateningly. The local company contacted the client's global resilience department, who in turn contacted us: could AS Solution get an agent on location to restore calm and deter any incident?

The solution: Rapid intervention and a steady hand

Our first order of business was to get a qualified agent on location as soon as possible. Best practice is clear on this point: it is critical to set up preventive measures quickly after a threat. Due to our network of vetted partners, we were able to get a qualified agent on the scene within an hour—despite the fact that this was on the other side of the country.

The agent has a well-defined role in cases like these: he is there to support the entire staff, make sure that they are safe, and allow everyone to relax and get back to work. After meeting with managers and getting a brief on the main issues, our agent blends into the background, but remains the primary line of defense should anything happen.

This kind of agent is trained in deterrence and prevention, but is also ready to initiate reactive procedures if necessary. As is typical, the agent we deployed that day was a former law enforcement officer with years of experience in deescalating conflicts; he also has close ties with local police to draw on for backup if needed.

The results: Minimal disruption gives another productive day at the office—and peace of mind

Our agent stayed on location for the day until staff went home. There were no further incidents that day. The disgruntled employee moved on, and so did the company.

Some might superficially conclude that this whole exercise was superfluous, and that there is no reason to increase readiness if nothing happens. We believe they miss the point.

In taking decisive action on real, perceived threats in the workplace, the client did its due diligence and then followed through. Initiating preventive protection in such circumstances is a clear expression of the company's perception of duty of care toward staff and managers, and very much in line with the kind of forward thinking that defines good executive protection—and a successful company.

Helping a client stay safe and make good decisions when all hell breaks loose

We provide secure travel logistics for our clients so they can maintain their productivity and well-being wherever their interests take them. While our managers and agents always train and prepare for the worst, in normal circumstances good planning and procedures allow us to provide our principals with seamless transportation and security that they hardly notice as they move about their day.

The November 2015 Paris attacks were anything but normal circumstances, however. As it happens, we were there with a client entourage when six separate terrorist attacks shook the French capital—and threw the city into a deep state of shock and near paralysis.

The challenge: Keep our client safe and on top of events in a rapidly deteriorating security environment

Our client, a U.S.-based corporation with operations world-wide, had planned a major conference in Paris for many months. In attendance were thousands of stakeholders from around Europe and the rest of the world as well as the company's top management.

When all hell broke loose on the evening of November 13 and terrorists killed 130 people, the conference was in full swing. The conference hotel was located between several of the attack locations.

In such chaotic circumstances the first priority is of course client safety. For us, in this case, that meant that the focus of our efforts was the company's top managers and their families. But accessing reliable information about what is happening quickly becomes critical, too, for without this, informed decisions are impossible. So the client asked us to use our local contacts to get all the information we could to enable better decision making.

The solution: Risk mitigation and avoidance—and intensive intelligence gathering

While our primary focus continued to be keeping our principals out of harm's way, intelligence gathering soon became essential as well.

Within half an hour Paris was rocked by six deadly assaults at locations across the city. No one knew whether these attacks were just the beginning or whether more would follow. Police closed some streets soon after, while others remained open. Information on what had happened and official responses emerged piecemeal through the night through social media posts and media reports.

Drawing on our contacts within Parisian police and the French government, we were able to stay ahead of the information curve to keep the client updated and enable timely, well-informed decisions.

The results: A shortened conference and a shaken but relieved client

Fortunately, none of the company's participants were hurt in one of the deadliest terror attacks in recent history.

As the night wore on and our intelligence gathering continued apace, the client decided to cancel the rest of the conference: general security and transportation were too unsure to risk sending thousands to a conference. Because we could combine information from our own sources with what was available through the media, the client was able to make this difficult decision calmly and based on the best available facts, and implement it in a controlled way.

Our principal decided to stay for the length of the originally planned trip. As much of Paris was locked down, including important Metro lines and buses, the client was able to make good use of the security drivers we had in place over the next few days—and the best out of a bad situation.

Arranging a trip on the fly to a restricted military airport in India

For our principals, the so-called work/life balance is different than that of many people. They work a lot, some would say constantly. They have a profound sense of purpose and truly enjoy what they do, so the distinctions between "business and pleasure" are seldom black and white.

The incredible productivity of our principals depends not only on good planning or isolated stretches of downtime, but also on an ability to combine days on end of hectic business activity with the capacity to smell the roses along the way. As this case illustrates, good international EP facilitates all of this.

The challenge: Arrange a private trip to a restricted Indian military airport within 12 hours

The day before our principal was scheduled to fly into Delhi for an intense round of meetings, a strong wish took hold: wouldn't it be great to see the Taj Mahal for the first time? The

194

chance of visiting this, one of the wonders of the world, seemed just too good to pass up.

With some massaging the team could free up most of a day, two days hence, from meetings. The rest seemed simple: they were traveling on the corporate jet and their U.S.-based travel team believed it would be no problem to fly from Delhi to Agra, where the Taj is located, and back in the same day. They called AS Solution to arrange for extra EP agents in Agra to be on the ground the day after next.

When AS Solution's Indian managers pointed out that the Agra Airport was also a military facility with restricted access for private aircraft—and did not issue landing permits for foreign-registered aircraft at all—the client's team remained confident that they would sort it out. After spending a day trying to do so, they called us back: Could AS Solution find a way that the principal and his entourage could fly in and out of Agra Airport—tomorrow? We had 24 hours to arrange everything, and a window of 12 hours to secure landing permits or cancel the trip.

The solution: Work the network as it's never been worked before

India is known for many things, from astounding cultural heritage to intense religious devotion and marvelous cuisine. Among international businesspeople, it also has something of a reputation for time-consuming bureaucracy and travel logistics that are variously described as "difficult" to "harrowing." This trip would prove to demonstrate the best and worst of all of the above.

As getting a foreign plane into Agra was out of the question, our first order of business was to charter an India-registered Gulfstream. That was the easy part. The more difficult task was getting a landing permit into Agra, a process that even in the best circumstances takes at least seven working days. By that point, we had less than 12 hours.

Using their networks in the aviation industry and government, AS Solution's Indian team was able to get a landing permit for the plane and its passengers on time—and without any funny business—and make the trip possible.

The results: A "miracle" behind the scenes and a great day for the client

The principal's group flew from Delhi to Agra the next morning and had an amazing day experiencing some of the best that India has to offer. In addition to extra security in Agra, we also arranged several types of ground transportation, an expert guide and a gourmet lunch. Everything went off without a hitch.

To this day, many within our Indian network, even those who helped us do it, still consider it miraculous that we managed to get the necessary flight permits. We know we can't make miracles happen every day, but we are convinced that the networks we maintain worldwide make them just a little more likely.

Quantum leap in intelligence analysis capacity within three months

Our executive protection services depend on up-to-date information to stay abreast of emerging risks to our principals wherever they might travel. So it's no wonder we rely on many sources—including our broad network of on-the-ground eyes, ears and minds—to predict, prevent and mitigate threats to our principals. Indeed, our most comprehensive executive protection programs have dedicated intelligence analysts as part of the team.

But intelligence analysis has a wide range of benefits that are applicable to other corporate objectives, too. Managers rely on intelligence reports to ensure the well-being of employees, business continuity, regulatory compliance, reputation and more. That is why intelligence analysis is a growing part of our business.

The challenge: Ramp up a corporate intelligence analysis program fast

Our client is a Fortune 500 corporation with global reach and a complex, international supply chain. An internal review determined that intelligence regarding their far-flung network of factories across a wide swath of emerging markets left much to be desired.

In addition to duty of care toward their thousands of employees traveling around the world every day, they realized the need to better understand the dynamic and interdependent effects that myriad issues—political, economic, climate-related, etc.—could have on their businesses at local, national, regional and global levels. The one intelligence analyst currently trying to keep an eye on developments in the nearly 50 countries where the company had manufacturing could not keep up.

The company's HR experts were not geared to this specialized niche, so they approached us with an ambitious brief and a tight deadline: Could AS Solution help the company set up a world-class corporate intelligence analysis program within three months?

The solution: Provide a top-notch talent pool and tailor-made training

After consulting with the client on program objectives and operations, we quickly set about identifying relevant talent profiles in order to provide the client with a good selection of carefully vetted candidates. Drawing on our network and industry insight—and with our intel experts working closely with the client and our recruitment manager—we were able to present the client with shortlists for each position, enabling the company to fill 10 new positions within three months.

In parallel with recruitment activities, we developed operational standards and a dedicated training program so that the new recruits could quickly gel into a team that delivered results. Two guiding principles were especially important here:

1. First, the program must live up to best practices within the intelligence analyst industry in order to deliver the highest standard of actionable intelligence in a consistently reliable way.

2. Second, the program must be a true expression of the company's unique culture and value set, for only in this way would it align with corporate practices and earn the influence which managers deemed so important for its success.

The results: A fully functioning program in months, not years

Recruitment began as soon as the client approved our recommendations, and ran from mid-May into June. Within weeks, we were able to present the first group of approved, vetted candidates that lived up to the client's and our demands. Onboarding was completed by August, when the first training sessions also took place.

The corporate intelligence analysis team now counts roughly a dozen analysts, and works as planned to provide departmental and divisional managers with timely reports that improve decision making across the company. We continue to provide training and consultancy as the program matures.

Multiple agendas, five countries, more than 25 high-level travelers? No problem.

At AS Solution, helping our clients get from A to B is something we put a lot of effort into.

Keeping them safe as they move around the country and the world is our first priority, of course. But smooth travel logistics does more than that. It allows our principals to make the most of their time wherever they go. By keeping their focus on running their business rather than running around looking for taxis, hotels and the next meeting, they get more done even when they are on the road.

Ultimately, our goal is replace the burden of travel with an experience that keeps them safe, productive—and even happy—when moving from A to B and beyond.

The challenge: Delivering comprehensive protection in a multi-country, multi-person itinerary

Our client, a high-profile chief executive at a high-profile Fortune 500 company, was planning a major trip that would take him to five countries spread throughout Asia.

In addition to a wide variety of meetings with subsidiaries and customers, our principal had also been invited to a number of tête-à-têtes with the highest level of government in the capitals he planned to visit. More than 25 company executives were also included in the itinerary, as they would be participating in key meetings and a number of off-site events. Finally, the CEO wanted to take a short personal vacation while in the region.

The solution: Leap-frogging agents and seamless integration of our own and partner resources

Drawing on a number of internal and external resources, we configured a team capable of delivering seamless secure travel across Asia.

The team integrated two groups: (1) our own executive protection agents who were already embedded in the client's organization and (2) in-country security and logistics providers. Full-time executive protection professionals already working for the client were designated as detail leaders.

The itinerary was complex. The first two countries each required support in two separate cities; in the final three countries, the entourage increased by up to 25 additional high-level travelers.

In order to provide the client with a consistent and familiar travel experience, we "leap-frogged" agents between destinations. Our staff did advance work at all stops to make sure that local assets were vetted and in place, and ready to deliver according to objectives.

We created a support matrix across the entire team so that everyone involved could easily understand the plan and their roles, ensuring reliable and efficient delivery.

The results: A highly successful trip for the client

The trip was highly successful for our client.

All travelers accomplished their planned goals, and we managed to stick to the ambitious itinerary despite a few unforeseen incidents. Our team easily handled the few minor illnesses that slowed down several company travelers. We quickly resolved a customs issue that interrupted the journey for one of our highest-level participants and could have turned into a frustrating experience.

Even though the itinerary was complex and complicated by the large entourage and the multiple agendas and destinations, the trip went off without a hitch.

Setting up, training and maintaining a covert executive protection and surveillance detection program to provide top-notch security—without anyone noticing

We regularly work with high net worth individuals, families and their offices. In many ways, the executive protection and security needs of these families are similar to those of corporations. After all, these high net worth individuals are often founders of highly successful companies, and in that sense share many characteristics with the C-suite principals for whom we typically provide executive protection.

In important ways, however, families are not the same as corporations, and neither are their protection needs. Parents would rather their children not notice the added security, as that might make them afraid. Affluent families are first and foremost families, and want to do what families do without extra people hovering about nearby. Interestingly, we see the same tendency in more and more corporations, who also are beginning to prefer a more covert protection style for their executives.

The challenge: Keep threats as far away from a prominent family—without bothering them about it

We were asked to provide a personal protection program for a prominent high net worth individual that integrated work-related executive protection with 24/7 protection of his family. In addition to the family's prominence, they had also received direct threats.

Our work began with an assessment that identified probable risks (hostile groups and individuals) and then matched these against a vulnerability evaluation of the principal and his family as they moved through their lives.

We then designed a protective program to optimize the family's security, and matched it to the family's lifestyle and personal preferences. It was here that this case becomes more than "just another executive protection program"—but in many ways a typical AS Solution project. The family just wanted to get on with its life as normally as possible, and did not want to be encumbered in any way, or noticed for its protection. In fact, they required that the executive protection program basically be invisible to family members as well as the press, colleagues and general public—and still highly effective.

The solution: Highly trained covert surveillance and protection teams

Based on the probable threats and vulnerabilities discovered in our Risk, Threat and Vulnerability Analysis (RTVA) process, we created a security master plan including all preventative and emergency procedures. This made for an effective protective program that plugs security vulnerabilities while maintaining the principals' feelings of freedom and privacy—all while being invisible to both the trained and untrained eye.

The solution is based on a combination of covert executive protection and surveillance detection teams. The covert executive protection team is tasked with staying "within the bubble," unnoticed by the family and anyone else, and looking out to identify threats as early as possible and to create time and distance between the threat and principals. The surveillance detection team is tasked with staying "outside the bubble," unnoticed by anyone at all, and looking in toward the bubble in order to observe who might be observing the principals—and relaying this information to the executive protection team as the result of data analysis or in real time; and in the instance of an actual hostile act, intercepting the perpetrators as soon as possible.

Once the tasks were defined, and not before, we helped hire suitable professionals for each specialist role. We even field-tested candidates to assess their integrity, ability to make decisions under pressure, and initiative. Team training has been a critical part of the program's success. After recruitment, the two teams completed two separate, task- specific foundation classes on a pass/fail basis.

The results: Powerful and nearly invisible protection

We are now well into program implementation, and are happy to report that we satisfy all principal and shareholder requirements. We have created two small yet highly specialized protective details consisting of quality men and women who perform truly covert executive protection and surveillance detection. This results in an effective security system that is unnoticed by the principals and the public eye.

The combination of the covert executive protection and surveillance detection teams is powerful, and gives us a tactical advantage that is exceptionally strong. With traditional overt executive protection, persons of interest can identify vulnerabilities in our visible protection in order to circumvent it and get to the target; when we combine covert executive protection with surveillance detection, the perpetrators don't see our protection, and our team can seemingly emerge out of thin air to surprise them and stop attacks earlier and farther away.

Quarterly, we deliver enrichment and refresher training for all team members to sharpen existing skills, add new skills and methods as operations require, and continue their professional development.

Fast reaction to major threat keeps employees secure

No matter how much forward thinking a company does, we are all sometimes surprised by a sudden turn of events.

It may be a competitor making a surprise move, civil unrest that balloons into a sweeping sociopolitical upheaval, or something as simple as a key employee getting in a car accident.

In 2014, a hostile group announced its intentions to harm the staff and interests of a major corporation thousands of miles away.

The challenge: Providing fast protection after a sudden, significant threat

Not content to issue a general threat, the group issued a string of communiqués that were increasingly abusive and worrisome.

It soon became apparent that the company's top executives in particular were prime targets.

After a reliable governmental agency corroborated the genuineness—and seriousness—of the group's messages, the company's director of security called us for support.

The solution: Immediate response and comprehensive protection

Given the seriousness of the threat, a rapid response to ensure employee security was critical:

- The project required near-immediate deployment of teams to provide 24/7 protection.

- Within 24 hours of the call, AS Solution executive protection agents were on-site and on-duty at the company's headquarters.

- Within days, we had put together and deployed a comprehensive covert protection detail designed to keep safe the company executives who were most prominent and at risk.

At the height of the project, AS Solution had dozens of executive protection professionals on the job. In addition to safeguarding the company's HQ and top executives locally, we also provided secure travel and logistics for the principals throughout Europe and the United States.

The results: Short-term safety, long-term solutions

First and foremost, the client's executives stayed safe, happy and productive while on our watch.

No security breaches or incidents were encountered at any location.

As part of our engagement, we helped the client develop a long-term, in-house solution designed to keep its employees secure from future threats.

Providing seamless security for a blockbuster international roadshow

Executive protection and event security are two core AS Solution services. Rapid response, smooth travel logistics and international expertise are another three core services that our clients rely on.

On most days, we're delivering some combination of these five elements somewhere in the world. In 2014, we delivered all of them and more in an intensive three-week international roadshow that launched the world's biggest-ever IPO.

The challenge: Provide complete security for a highly ambitious IPO roadshow

A leading global company was preparing its much-anticipated initial public offering (IPO), which many observers predicted would result in the largest valuation ever seen.

210

In order to introduce the company to investors, the company planned an international roadshow that matched the scale of the stock offering. Key members of the executive team were packing their bags for a trip that would take them around the world, to more than a dozen cities in half a dozen countries, in a three-week whirlwind.

The company needed protection for its CEO and other execs as they traveled around the globe. This included secure transportation to and from all venues and event security at the investor meetings, as well as a range of other deliverables and security consulting. They asked AS Solution, one of the few companies in the world capable of delivering a project of such breadth and depth, to join the show.

Could AS Solution provide integrated executive protection, event security and security consulting for the entire international roadshow?

The solution: One of the most massive, tightly coordinated security projects we've ever handled

Against a tight timeline—and after a short planning phase that brought together many of our security experts from around the globe—we quickly began to organize the team that would keep the roadshow secure.

Over the course of the three-week project, the AS Solution team provided more than 320 days of vehicles and drivers, 240 days of venue security agents, 12 venue security sweeps, and 240 executive protection agent days.

We had a large security contingent at each venue, and we ensured investor meetings were safe by securing them comprehensively prior to and during the meetings.

We established secure communication lines with our own proven equipment. Our intelligence analysts prepared daily reports on the IPO roadshow's overall security situation, as well as local briefs for our team in every country and city that the road-show visited.

The logistical and organizational requirements of keeping one or two steps ahead of the roadshow to do pre-event security, combined with the ongoing secure travel and event security, were complex but doable. In all, we provided security to, from and in 12 cities: Abu Dhabi, Dubai, Baltimore, Boston, Chicago, Hong Kong, Kansas City, Kuwait, London, Los Angeles, New York, San Francisco and Singapore.

The results: The world's biggest-ever IPO—and no one ever noticed security

Most importantly, the client was safe, happy and productive during the entire roadshow. There were no security breaches or incidents.

The IPO went off without a hitch. As predicted, it proved to be the largest in history.

Tell us what's happening in an area cut off from all communications—and get our guy out if necessary

Hurricane Odile was the most powerful storm ever to hit Mexico's Baja Peninsula. When she swept across the Cabo San Lucas resort area in September 2014, Odile packed winds of up to 125 mph (200 km/hr) and dumped more than 12 inches (320 mm) of rain.

The exceptionally violent storm wreaked havoc across the tourist region. Flooding was extensive, windows in hotels and homes shattered like eggshells, and falling trees and power poles crippled communications. The area was completely without drinking water and power for days. Approximately 30,000 tourists were driven out of their hotels and rental homes.

The challenge: Find a client's executive in the middle of an area cut off from the rest of the world

At the height of the storm, no one outside of Los Cabos knew what was going on—except that things were very bad. The storm had effectively cut off the area from the rest of the world.

As the storm was peaking, the security director of one of our Fortune 500 clients contacted us. One of their executives and a friend were last heard of at 10 pm on September 15: the house they were staying in was heavily damaged, they had a few bottles of water and some peanuts but no electricity, transportation or running water.

Could AS Solution find out what was going on in Los Cabos, and how to evacuate the executive and his friend if necessary?

The solution: Work the network, then escalate as necessary

After several unsuccessful attempts to reach our usual contacts in Los Cabos—security directors at high-end hotels and top-ranking members of the local police—we escalated communication to another level, a senior military officer we know in Mexico. Our contact was able to open up a communication link with the Mexican military on the ground in Los Cabos, providing us with real-time local intelligence.

In less than an hour, we were able to inform our client what was happening on the ground. We could confirm that there had not been any deaths, and relate that the military and police were safeguarding tourists in shelters. Tourist evacuations had already begun, and local authorities were working around the clock to restore power and communications to the devastated area. We then provided our client with three evacuation and support options.

The results: The exec was located—and was fortunately fine

Fortunately, our travelers were unharmed and could be evacuated by the Mexican government shortly after the storm ended.

The incident confirms the value of maintaining a strong local network. We were able to get critical information out of Los Cabos long before the newswires knew what was going on, and were ready to evacuate if necessary. When normal communications are down, having another way to connect can go a long way to providing our clients with peace of mind.

Board-mandated executive protection program: Establishing the decision criteria

Increasingly, corporate boards are considering executive protection programs for their top executives—and they are asking their chief security officers a number of tough questions.

Do we need an executive protection program for our principals? Which criteria should we use to make the decision? Can we benchmark executive protection with other companies? If we do decide to mandate it, what should such a program include, and what are our options for setting up the program?

Unlike many other corporate decisions, the path to a board-mandated executive protection program is not something you learn about in business school. Corporate security officers and managers are hard-pressed to recommend the right executive protection program, and they sometimes find it difficult to discuss the importance of executive protection with their principals and the principals' staffs. Here's what one company did to better understand their options.

The challenge: Help the board of directors understand what executive protection is—and whether their principals needed it

We were referred to the chief security officer of a Fortune 500 company whose board was considering an executive protection program for its key executives.

Before mandating such a program, the board wanted to learn more about what an executive protection program actually is, which alternatives it should study when deciding the character of the program, how it could be organized, and of course, how much it would cost.

The chief security officer asked us, on a consultant basis, to lay out its options.

Could AS Solution prepare a report that would allow the board to decide whether or not—and how—to mandate an executive protection program?

The solution: A clear report that outlined the options, benefits and costs

Based on our experience with other Fortune 500 companies in related industries, we were able to create an overview that described best practice and common practices—and the difference between them. We described the various elements of a solid executive protection program, how each of the elements adds value to the organization, and how they work together in a systematic approach.

We outlined a number of alternative solutions and examined the budget consequences of each alternative. We developed a full set of options, including organizational charts, key performance indicators (KPIs) and customizations for implementing the alternatives incrementally or all at once.

The report also illustrated the importance of managing expectations and relationships between the principals, their support staff and other corporate departments in order to best set up the organization for success.

The results: Decisions based on facts, not preconceived notions

The report facilitated well-informed discussions between the board, the relevant principals and the corporate security organization.

The chief security officer now has a clear idea of his options in setting up a viable executive protection program. The board has the information it needs in order to make a decision about mandating such a program. And the principals are better able to express their expectations and demands regarding a protection program.

Even philanthropists need to stay safe

We have provided safe travel and other services for a number of philanthropic organizations over the years.

In terms of objectives, these projects are quite similar to any other executive protection program we deliver: Our goal is to keep the principals and others in their entourages safe, happy and productive wherever their travels take them.

In terms of style, however, corporate and nongovernmental organization (NGO) clients can be different. Travels with philanthropic organizations often take us far off the beaten track in developing countries into areas where few tourists or foreign business execs ever venture. And even though our primary objective is to keep our principals safe, most of them are not happy if security means setting up militaristic barriers between them and the people they are trying to help.

The challenge: Get an NGO group through the murder capital of the world—and then onto the back roads

One of our U.S.-based philanthropic clients wanted to take a group of stakeholders to Honduras. On the itinerary was San Pedro Sula, the unofficial murder capital of the world, as well as hundreds of miles of travel through remote rural areas.

In order for their travel guests to experience the people of Honduras firsthand, our client insisted that the communities they visited found them approachable while we kept them safe.

For this particular trip, the group would be spending most of its time in remote regions of Honduras, in rural areas with few paved roads—and during the rainy season.

The solution: A tailor-made mix of local expertise and resources

Working with tight monetary and time constraints, we put together a team of AS Solution security managers with the right mix of skills, Central American experience and personality. This core team was tasked with sourcing additional local resources—both personnel and vehicles—and with carrying out advance work to ensure that the logistics and security plan would deliver on all objectives.

All of our locally sourced Honduran travel security managers spoke Spanish and English and had training in field medical care. In addition to these security managers, we also identified and vetted local armed security who had the training to handle worst-case scenarios and were capable of blending unobtrusively into the environment.

As budgets did not allow for the latest model Land Rovers, we worked locally to source a number of vehicles that could keep our entourage moving safely and relatively comfortably through back roads.

The results: A safe trip in a tricky region

Our combined team of U.S. and Honduran travel security managers successfully managed logistics over hundreds of miles of remote highways, dirt roads and mountain paths without any security incidents.

In addition to navigating police checkpoints and muddy roads, our joint team helped the travelers manage a range of preexisting health conditions while roughing it in the countryside. They responded appropriately to a variety of travel illnesses, minor vehicle accidents and wilderness-related injuries.

Most importantly for our client, the travelers were able to enjoy a once-in-a-lifetime experience that brought them up close and personal with the rural communities which the philanthropic organization serves—all while staying safe and secure.

AS Solution continues to support these trips, and the client has now committed to a long-term contract that will allow many other groups to enjoy the same experience.

Turning around an executive protection program that was in trouble

We talk to a number of companies large and small about executive protection programs every week. Sometimes, the conversation starts something like this: "Executive protection? Yeah, we tried that a few times, but it didn't really work out for us, so we gave up the program."

At times, the conversation ends there. There are other times when this makes for the beginning of a great dialogue.

The challenge: The principals can't stand the current executive protection program—and want out

A Fortune 500 company approached us because they were not satisfied with the management and execution of their executive protection program. The company's board of directors had mandated a robust protection program for several of its top executives, all prominent figures in an industry that gets a lot of media attention, but program results were far from the board's requirements.

The principals were frustrated with the program's design and execution. Three program managers, all without the appropriate experience, had been put in charge and had left. The executive protection team members were overworked. At a time when its worldwide responsibilities were growing fast, corporate security management was spending more than 50 percent of its time dealing with executive protection team issues—much more than it should be.

The solution: Identify the problem, ensure program integrity ASAP, then plan for long-term sustainability

Our initial analysis identified the key problems, outlined a number of options and prioritized which improvements should be implemented first.

We discovered that the existing program lacked consistency, flexibility and scalability. There were no documented standard operating procedures. The readiness of their executive protection team members was discouragingly low, and the team's professional development was nonexistent.

Working closely with the client, one of the first things we did was to provide full-time, contracted support personnel to ensure that the program met the requirements of the board mandate as soon as possible. Drawing on our pool of vetted, experienced executive protection professionals, we were quickly able to pull together team members who fit the principals' lifestyle, corporate culture and security requirements.

In addition to staff, we also provided a full-time, contracted executive protection director to stabilize the program. Given the history of previous executive protection efforts, it was essential to establish the right partnerships within the company and to nurture relationships with a number of key stakeholders.

While our executive protection strategy was written to address all foreseeable requirements, its implementation was designed to be flexible. Our recommendations were accompanied by a range of options so that the client could proceed at a pace that best suited its needs and budget.

That's why the standard operating procedures that we created included documenting and training the entire team. We helped the client hire all the full-time executive protection team members, including a new executive protection manager, and develop career paths and performance management tools for them.

The results: A fully functioning executive program that the principals like

As mandated by the board, we have now put in place a fully functioning executive protection program to protect the corporation's principals. The program is flexible and scalable, and there are strategies to serve additional principals at home or abroad as needs arise.

Importantly, we have been able to develop trusted relationships between the executive protection team, the client's principals and their immediate staff, and the client's corporate security management and other related departments.

We continue to provide full-time, senior-level, strategic advising and consulting to the company's executive protection manager, global security manager, principals and their support staff.

Index